for **BANJO**

T0078804

ACKNOWLEDGMENTS

Lydia Sylvia would like to thank "Crazy-Hair" Chris Foy and the Martin/Songco/Summers family for their support. She also would like to thank Walt Michael, Scott Ainslie, Guy Davis, Dom Flemons and everyone at Common Ground on the Hill who has helped to preserve and celebrate traditional blues music.

Dave Rubin thanks Jeff Schroedl, Kurt Plahna, Jim Schustedt and everyone at Hal Leonard, along with Zeke Schein, Eli Smith and Edward Komara. In addition, he would like to acknowledge Eric LeBlanc, the world famous blues, jazz and popular music expert, for his invaluable assistance and friendship, as well as Peter Szego, the renowned banjo expert and collector, for his help and encouragement early on in the project.

Robert Johnson Studio Portrait

Hooks Bros., Memphis, c. 1935

© 1989 Delta Haze Corporation

All Rights Reserved. Used By Permission.

Arrangements by Lydia Sylvia and Jim Schustedt

ISBN 978-1-4803-0008-8

HAL•LEONARD®
CORPORATION
7777 W. BLUEMOUND RD. P.O. BOX 13819 MILWAUKEE, WI 53213

Visit Hal Leonard Online at
www.halleonard.com

PREFACE

The fame and infamy of Robert Johnson (1911–1938) has grown to the level of myth. The former rests firmly on his virtuosic musical accomplishments predicated on summing up virtually all that had transpired previously in the prewar country music era 1926–1936, and his very real powers as an "American griot" creating haunting tales with striking poetic lyrics. The latter concerns the supposed selling of his soul to the devil at the crossroads in exchange for his vaunted ability, in a tale promulgated in the 1960s. As famously quoted in *The Man Who Shot Liberty Valance*: "When the legend becomes fact, print the legend."

The undeniable "fact" that his songs are a great technical challenge for guitarists to play accurately is borne out by the many cover versions simplified for practical rather than aesthetic reasons. For the most reliable note-for-note reference source, however, check out *Robert Johnson: The New Transcriptions* (Hal Leonard Corporation). The banjo precedes the guitar in the evolution of the blues and by all accounts Robert Johnson did not play one. Until now, no attempt has been made to arrange a wide selection of his music for the instrument. The form and spirit of Robert Johnson's original recordings are faithfully captured in these 15 arrangements while incorporating the unique sonic qualities of the 5-string banjo. The results are a heretofore unavailable opportunity for banjo players to experience the immense satisfaction of performing the music of one of the greatest legends of the blues.

Dave Rubin
NYC

CONTENTS

THE BANJO IN THE BLUES
By Dave Rubin

Just as the blues is the glorious original American music gestated in the South after the Civil War via the commingling of the African and Anglo cultures, so, too, the banjo is the native instrument. With roots in Africa to the five-string Gambian "akonting," among other instruments, and called the "mbanza" in the Bantu/Kimbundo language, it was brought over in the transatlantic slave trade in the 18th century. Nicholas Cresswell, a British visitor to the colonies around the time of the Revolutionary War, wrote in his journal of 1774 about going to a "Negro Ball" and seeing the slaves dance to the music of the "banjor," and later attending a barbecue where the banjo and fiddle were played. None other an authority on slavery than Thomas Jefferson stated "The instrument proper to them is the banjar, which they brought hither from Africa, and which is the origin of the guitar, its chords [strings] being precisely the four lower chords [strings] of the guitar." Also called the "banza," "bangil," "banjer," "banger," "banjaw," "banjie," "bandore" and "strum-strum," they were initially constructed from hollowed out gourds, stretched animal skins and sticks for a neck.

By 1843 and the official debut of the first minstrel show, the banjo had been appropriated by the white population and was more substantially constructed from solid wood and metal parts. The skin head could thus be pulled tighter against the rim, resulting in a louder, higher pitched sound. Eventually the virulent racism associated with minstrelsy, in addition to the brighter sound and shorter sustain when compared to the earlier slack, lower pitch of the previous instruments favored for self-accompaniment, caused the banjo to fall out of favor with many African-Americans. When guitars left behind in the South by Union soldiers following the Civil War found their way into the hands of black musicians, however, it had the greatest impact on the early development of the blues circa the 1880s and beyond. By the turn of the 20th century, the rising popularity of both the blues and the guitar would contribute to the demise of the blues banjo.

The relatively few pre-WWII blues banjoists of note include Vivian "Sam" Chatmon of the legendary Chatmon clan, Papa Charlie Jackson and Gus Cannon of the Memphis Jug Band. Chatmon (1900–1983), who helped popularize the immortal "Sittin' on Top of the World" while with his brothers in the Mississippi Sheiks, stated that he began playing tenor banjo circa 1916, tuning it to the bottom four strings of the guitar and performing with it and the "bull fiddle" and guitar.

Following the debut of "Crazy Blues" by Mamie Smith in 1920, the era of recorded blues commenced and record labels eventually realized the potential audience for country blues, starting with Blind Lemon Jefferson in 1926. Though the banjo would rarely be the featured instrument, Papa Charlie Jackson (1887–1938) managed to have a substantial recording career on a 6-string banjo-guitar beginning in 1924 as the first male singer/"guitarist" to record a commercially successful blues with "Papa's Lawdy Lawdy Blues" b/w "Airy Man Blues." He became popular playing very much in the accompaniment style associated with banjo blues at that time. His most famous compositions are "Salty Dog Blues," "Spoonful" and "Shake That Thing" and he is acknowledged as one of the creators of the ribald "hokum" music.

Gus Cannon (1884–1979) was arguably the greatest blues banjoist and likely the most recorded. While still a child he constructed a homemade banjo from a frying pan and a coonskin. As a young man in Clarksdale he was shown how to play slide guitar with a knife and adapted the technique to the banjo. Cannon began recording in 1927 as "Banjo Joe" with Blind Blake on guitar and the same year he waxed the amazing "Poor Boy, Long Ways from Home" containing his innovative slide work. However, he would achieve broader fame as the leader of Cannon's Jug Stompers in Memphis. Their "Jonestown Blues" from 1929 shows him embellishing with sophisticated single-note lines on the banjo in the manner of Blind Lemon Jefferson. Far from a gourd and stick or a frying pan, his instruments of choice were an Orpheum and Gretsch Broadkaster. Unfortunately, Cannon and his group did not record after 1930 and he performed sporadically into the early 1960s. In 1963, however, the Rooftop Singers cut a version of his "Walk Right In" from 1929 and scored a No. 1 hit in the folk music and "hootenanny" era. The notoriety and royalties afforded him a second shot at a career after economic straits had previously forced him to pawn his banjo, and he would go on to play in public and record for years afterward.

Moran Lee "Dock" Boggs (1898–1971) was a coal miner who also began recording in 1927 and combined Appalachian folk music and African-American blues on the banjo. Fascination with the black string bands he heard in Virginia led to his absorbing their picking technique on the banjo as opposed to the "frailing" style heard in his community. His career was essentially over by 1931, but he was rediscovered in the '60s folk boom and recorded for Folkways Records. His "Sugar Baby" and "Country Blues" both appear on Harry Smith's hugely influential 1951 *Anthology of American Folk Music.*

Concurrently with the phasing out of the banjo in the blues by the 1930s, the swing jazz bands of the era likewise began featuring guitarists. Duke Ellington was the first to make the change in his orchestra, with his banjo man Fred Guy going to tenor guitar and then a Gibson L-5 arch top. Soon other groups followed suit. Guitar companies took notice and began producing tenor guitars tuned, low to high, C–G–D–A like a tenor banjo in order to make the transition easier for banjoists.

Though blues banjo had all but died out as a commercial entity after WWII, one significant exception was in the supremely talented hands of Rev. Gary Davis (1896–1972). The legendary virtuoso finger-style blues, gospel and ragtime guitarist recorded a series of albums beginning in the early 1960s featuring a 6-string Decring banjo tuned exactly like a guitar in standard. Also known as a "banjitar," it may be heard on *The Blues Guitar and Banjo of Rev. Gary Davis* (Prestige 7725).

In the new millennium many dedicated blues musicians, along with passionate organizations, keep the banjo vital in their music. Canadian Kevin "Harry Manx" MacKenzie (b. 1955), born on the Isle of Mann, offers a unique combination of Western and Eastern music by mixing country slide guitar blues and traditional classical Indian ragas in a revolutionary hybrid he terms "Mysticsippi." Playing guitar, six-string banjo and the 20-stringed Mohan Veena that he studied in India with its inventor, Vishna Mohan Bhatt, Manx has recorded 12 albums, the latest being "Om Suite Ohm," whose title reveals his wry sense of humor.

Guy Davis (b. 1952), the son of Ruby Dee and Ossie Davis, has been one of the leading standard bearers for traditional country blues, pre-blues black music and his own original idiomatic compositions for over a quarter of a century. Since 1978 he has released 12 albums while also having a side career as a screen and stage actor and receiving prestigious awards in both areas of his art. He is a versatile instrumentalist on guitar, harmonica, bass, keyboards, percussion and banjo. The latter may be prominently heard to great expressive effect on his creative cover of "Po' Boy, Great Long Ways from Home" by Blind Willie McTell and the original "Shaky Pudding" on *Skunkmello*, along with the original "Slow Motion Daddy" and a cover of "Can't Be Satisfied" on *Sweetheart Like You.*

James "Sparky" Rucker (b. 1946) and his wife Rhonda both sing and play guitar and banjo in addition to other instruments. The most frequently cited of their nine albums together is *The Blue & Grey in Black & White* containing their evocative, moving versions of Civil War songs from the North and the South. However, *Heroes & Hard Times: Black American Ballads and Story Songs* focuses on his chosen role as a keeper of the historic black oral tradition in song, along with the blues as heard on *Bound to Sing the Blues* and *Cold and Lonesome Train*, among others. The Ruckers' *Treasures & Tears* was nominated for a Handy award in 1991.

The uncontested leading contemporary advocate for reclaiming the banjo as an African-American instrument is Chicago-born Otis Taylor (b. 1948). Since 1996 he has released 13 groundbreaking albums of what he calls "trance blues" performed on the electric solidbody banjo, in addition to guitar, mandolin and harmonica, while addressing the history of racism with uncompromising candor. His latest album, *My World Is Gone*, was released in 2013. The Telarc Records artist has been the recipient of numerous awards from the Blues Foundation and *Down Beat* magazine and began the annual Otis Taylor Trance Blues Festival in Boulder, Colorado in 2010.

THE SONGS
By Dave Rubin

CROSS ROAD BLUES (CROSSROADS)

As one of the iconic Robert Johnson songs, "Cross Road Blues (Crossroads)" has been covered as a blues-rock classic by Cream on *Wheels of Fire* and willfully misinterpreted to support the myth that Johnson sold his soul to the devil at the crossroads in Mississippi in exchange for other-worldly instrumental skills. Bursting with dynamic syncopation derived from piano blues and featuring slashing slide licks, the banjo arrangement benefits from the relatively short sustain and piercing timbre of the instrument.

DRUNKEN HEARTED MAN

Along with "Malted Milk," one of two songs Johnson based on the music of Lonnie Johnson (no relation), originally in drop-D tuning. The emphasis of the sound of the banjo in the upper register perfectly complements the solo country blues style of Lonnie Johnson as filtered through Robert Johnson.

FROM FOUR UNTIL LATE

Reminiscent of the ragtime guitar style of Blind Blake and also covered by Cream on *Fresh Cream*, it is in the key of C as opposed to the more common Delta blues guitar keys of E, A, G and D. The lyric "From Memphis to Norfolk is a thirty-six hour's ride," a span of 800 miles, may sound like an excessively slow trip until one realizes the modest horsepower of cars in 1936 and the lack of an interstate highway system.

HELL HOUND ON MY TRAIL

One of the songs that contributed to the devil myth and the belief that Johnson was a tortured soul. It is more likely, however, that he knew the fears and suspicions of his audience and was playing into them for effect and his popularity. His Em tuning, borrowed from Skip James, only adds to the dark musical ambience complementing the scarifying lyrics, proof positive that Steve Martin was wrong when he said a sad song could not be played on the banjo.

I BELIEVE I'LL DUST MY BROOM

Along with "Sweet Home Chicago," the most famous and influential Johnson composition. Antecedents may be found in previous piano blues, but Johnson arrived at a unique and unusual Aadd9 "devil tuning" to accommodate his guitar conception. The 1951 electric guitar version in open D by Elmore James has influenced virtually every blues and countless rock slide guitarists.

I'M A STEADY ROLLIN' MAN (STEADY ROLLIN' MAN)

A classic shuffle tune originally in standard tuning on the guitar. Another exceptional banjo arrangement also functioning as a superb tutorial in "Country Blues 101."

KIND HEARTED WOMAN BLUES

The only recorded Johnson song to feature a guitar solo. The banjo tuning and arrangement faithfully replicates the rich harmony, dynamics and supple swing of the original.

LOVE IN VAIN BLUES

Famously covered by the Rolling Stones on *Let It Bleed*, the original is the only Johnson song in the common country blues tuning of open G.

ME AND THE DEVIL BLUES

Yet another reference to "Old Scratch" has added to the supernatural aura surrounding Johnson promoted by many fans and writers. His composition gives a nod to the piano blues of Leroy Carr and features his signature dominant triple-stops and diminished triads on the upper strings.

RAMBLIN' ON MY MIND

Covered by Eric Clapton on *Blues Breakers, John Mayall with Eric Clapton*, later in his solo career, and on the CD/DVD version of *Me and Mr. Johnson*. The original stands as a fine introduction to playing fretted boogie patterns in conjunction with slide licks and the banjo arrangement likewise teaches aspiring blues banjoists the same enviable and versatile skills.

STOP BREAKIN' DOWN BLUES

Covered by Junior Wells on *Coming at You* and the Rolling Stones on *Exile on Main St.* a classic Johnson boogie shuffle with his signature open A tuning licks moving harmonically from I to I7. Arranged on the banjo for maximum momentum and deep groove.

SWEET HOME CHICAGO

The most-covered Johnson classic and the blueprint for numerous blues and rock that followed via its landmark chugging boogie shuffle rhythm. Notice the inventive, intelligent way the pattern was arranged for the banjo.

THEY'RE RED HOT

Pure hokum! Johnson flashes his "hot" comping chops with hip triads and triple-stops filled out with 4-string voicings to show he could compete with his peers. The banjo arrangement is just as cool with the quick attack and quick decay of the instrument complementing the staccato rush of chords.

32-20 BLUES

The original is a virtuoso performance by a virtuoso blues guitarist. The preponderance of pumping quarter notes are reproduced in the banjo arrangement for a propulsive groove that is as challenging as it is rewarding.

WALKIN' BLUES

With roots in work songs and specifically Son House's "My Black Mama," Johnson crafted a timeless blues that evokes the indomitable spirit, pathos and power of the emotionally charged genre. The twang of the banjo accentuates the sharp slide licks in between the "chop" of the bass notes.

PERFORMANCE NOTES
By Jim Schustedt

If you have an electronic tuner, you'll get your money's worth while using this book. If you don't already have one, buy one. You'll need it to navigate through these arrangements. If you're an experienced bluegrass banjo player, you'll quickly realize that there is nothing bluegrassy about these arrangements. This is by design. To sound like Robert Johnson, you have to play like Robert Johnson. Robert's guitar style consists of foundational rhythm vamps, and high-note licks interspersed between the lyric phrases. First-time listeners often think they're hearing two guitarists on the old recordings, but indeed it was just Robert. In this era the vocal and guitar were recorded live, with no overdubs or multi-tracking.

There are several different tunings used for these arrangements. Robert utilized several unique tunings on his guitar, and thus we must take the same approach here to capture the essence of his songs. There is a tuning chart at the end of this section so you'll be able to easily locate other songs in the same or similar tunings. To match the pitch of the recordings, you'll need to detune a half-step for some songs, for others you'll need to capo. If you don't already own a capo, you'll need to buy one. This means you'll need a way to capo your 5th string as well. One style of 5th-string capo consists of a rail that is screwed to the side of the neck parallel to the 5th string. A small clamp slides along the rail that depresses the string at the desired fret. Although this style of capo works fine, it can interfere with your fret-hand thumb. In my opinion, a better alternative is the model railroad spike. If you can't find them at your local music store, they're available at most hobby shops that sell electric trains. "O" gauge spikes are the preferred size. Be sure to have them installed by someone who has had prior experience performing this operation, especially if you have an expensive instrument. Installation entails driving the spikes into tiny, pre-drilled holes at various locations in the fretboard. The heads of the spikes stand proud above the fretboard to allow the player to hook the 5th string under the head of the appropriate spike, which causes the string to maintain contact with the fret.

These arrangements will sound best when picked with bare fingers due to muting techniques, but thumbpick and fingerpicks will also work fine if you find it awkward to go pickless. Every note in the transcription includes pick-hand fingerings below the tab. These banjo arrangements correspond to the *Robert Johnson: The Complete Recordings* audio, and you'll be best served if you purchase a copy. Most of his songs are blues shuffles in 4/4 time, but Robert often added or subtracted beats at will, often several times in each verse. The large time signature numbers on the tab staff will alert you when there is a meter change. Many of these banjo arrangements employ repeat signs around Verse sections. Robert often varied his guitar parts on subsequent verses, both harmonically and rhythmically, so feel free to change thing up a bit. Once you've digested several of these songs you'll have accumulated an arsenal R.J. licks that you'll be able to interject at will.

The performance notes for each song will help you get in tune, introduce you to notation symbols and techniques, and give you specific fingering for some of the more difficult licks. Often the information is vital for playing the arrangement properly. The performance notes chronicle the first time the technique or notation is used in the book. This information may be pertinent for the other songs, so if you decide to jump ahead to your favorite song, take time to read all the performance notes first. At the back of the book is a Banjo Notation Legend, which will explain rhythmic note and rest values, how *D.S. al Codas* work, as well as hammer-ons, pull-offs, slides and chokes. Enjoy!

Cross Road Blues (Crossroads)

This arrangement is based on "take 2" of the recording. This song is in standard G tuning, but you'll need to capo at the 4th fret to play along with the recording. Likewise, you'll need to capo the 5th string four frets above its starting point, at the 9th fret. This song also requires the use of a slide. Often called "bottlenecks," they are made of glass, brass, chromed steel, or ceramic. Get one that fits loosely on the pinky of your fret hand. Rest the slide on the strings, but don't press down hard. You don't want it to touch the fretboard or the frets. It's important to lay the slide directly above the metal fret so the notes will be in tune. Wiggling the slide will make the notes sustain a bit more and will add vibrato. The wavy line above the staff is the symbol used to indicate vibrato.

To the far right of the tempo marking, located above the first measure of the song, is the shuffle, or swing feel, indicator. This parenthetical information tells you to alter the duration of the eighth notes in the song. When you see two consecutive eighths, play the first note longer and the second note shorter than normal. The first should be sustained the combined duration of the first two notes of an eighth-note triplet. The second eighth note will be sustained the same as the last note of an eighth-note triplet. This long-short shuffle rhythm is used in all but one song in this book.

The arrows to the left of the tab numbers indicate to strum the strings. The upward-pointing arrows in measure 3 of the song tell you to start with your thumbpick on the 4th string and, in one motion, pick the 4th and 3rd strings. You'll notice it's actually a downward strum on the banjo if you're right handed.

In measure 7 of the Verse, barre your index finger at the 5th fret, then fret and choke (push up) the 1st string, 8th fret with your ring finger. You want to raise the pitch only a quarter step.

Drunken Hearted Man

This arrangement is based on the "take 1" recording. Before you start playing, be sure to tune your banjo as indicated. If you're in G tuning, raise the pitch of the first string to E, then raise the pitch of the 5th string to A. You'll need to capo at the 1st fret to match the recording. Be sure to capo your 5th string at the 6th fret. If you're nervous about breaking the 5th string while trying to tuning it to A, leave it tuned to G and capo the 5th string at the 8th fret, 3 frets above the tuning machine.

Fret the first note of the song with your pinky and keep it planted until the hammer-on in the second full measure. For the D7 chord in the first measure, use your middle finger to fret the 10 on the 4th string, and your ring finger for the 10 on the 2nd string. For the G chord that follows, use your index finger for the 7 on the 3rd string. When the G chord changes from major to minor, use your middle finger for the 8 on the 4th string. Then, after the hammer-on, barre your index finger at the 7th fret. Move the barre to the 2nd fret for the A7 chord during the eighth rest on the "and" of beat 1.

The small dot above the tab numbers of the D chord in measure 3 of the Intro is called a *staccato*. Play the notes shorter than normal when you see one. This can be performed two different ways: 1) immediately after picking the strings, release a bit of pressure of your fretting fingers but don't lift off all the way; 2) touch the strings with your picking hand immediately after plucking the strings. When there are staccatoed open strings, you'll need to go with option 2.

From Four Until Late

Using standard G tuning as your point of reference, tune the 1st string up a whole step to E, and lower the 4th string down a whole step to C. For the first measure and a half of the Intro, barre your index finger across the first four strings at the 8th fret. Barre again at the 1st fret for the F and F minor chords in the 3rd measure; likewise in the 5th and 6th measures of the Verse. In measure 7 of the Verse, use your index finger to fret the last note. This will put your left hand in the position to play the notes in measure 8. Switch to your middle finger to fret the doublestops on the 2nd fret of the 3rd and 4th strings in the 9th measure.

Above measure 5 of the second Verse section is the directive "4th time, w/ Fill1." This means substitute the two measures that are written in the Fill box at the bottom of the page during the 5th Verse. Rejoin the Verse at the C chord.

Hell Hound on My Trail

With G tuning as your point of reference, raise your 1st and 4th strings up a whole step to E, then lower your 5th string to E. The recording is about a quarter-step sharp, so you'll need to twist the pegs a bit higher to play along with the recording.

The trickiest move in the song is beat 1 of measure 4 of the Intro. Use your middle finger to fret the 2nd string, 2nd fret, and then hammer your index and ring fingers simultaneously – index on the 3rd string, 1st fret; ring on the 2nd string, 3rd fret. Notice the quarter-step chokes in the first few measures of the Verse. Fret the double stops with your index and middle fingers on the 1st and 2nd strings respectively, then push (choke) the 2nd string upward slightly while your index stays planted.

I Believe I'll Dust My Broom

We're using an unusual tuning for this one. From standard G tuning, raise the pitch of the 3rd string a whole step to A, and lower the 5th string to E. Then capo strings 4 through 1 at the 2nd fret. With the capo in position, the pitches of the 5th and 1st strings will be identical. The 5th string should not be capoed for this song. Since the tuning and capoing is so unusual, we haven't included two sets of chord symbols as we normally do when capos are employed.

In measure 7, barre your index finger at the 5th fret, then use your middle finger to fret the 3rd string at the 7th fret for beats 2 and 4. This will allow you to use your ring finger at the 8th fret for the last note of the measure, and your pinky at the 9th fret for the first note of measure 8. This measure is a bit tricky; master the steady rhythm with the thumb before trying to add the top notes with your middle and index fingers.

I'm a Steady Rollin' Man
(Steady Rollin' Man)

This arrangement is in standard G tuning, but you'll need to capo the 2nd fret to play along with the recording. Capo the 5th string two frets up as well.

Use your middle finger to fret the first note. This will position your index finger to fret the 6th fret of the 2nd string and your pinky to fret the 9th fret of the 1st string on beat 1 of measure 1. Slide this whole chord shape down one fret at beat 3, and then add your ring finger on the 2nd string, 7th fret for the "and" of beat 3. Use your ring finger again for the choke on beat 2 of the next measure. While picking the open 3rd string at the end of the 2/4 bar, shift your fret hand down and prepare to fret the 5th fret of the 1st string with your pinky. Your index and middle fingers will be poised to fret the 4th and 2nd strings respectively.

In measures 5 and 6 of the Verse, barre your index finger at the 5th fret. Likewise barre at the 7th fret in measure 9.

Watch for the syncopated rhythm (eighth-quarter-eighth, eighth-quarter-eighth) in measure 2 of the 5th ending. The fingering is a bit of a stretch, too.

Kind Hearted Woman Blues

This arrangement is based on "take 1" of the recording. From standard G tuning as your point of reference, tune the 2nd string down to A, then capo at the 4th fret. (Capo the 5th string four frets up, too.)

In the Intro there are several reverse strums indicated by a downward-pointing arrow. Drag your pick-hand index finger across the 1st and 2nd strings. There is a more deliberate reverse strum in measure 3 of the Intro, indicated by the wavy arrow. For this one, drag your finger a bit slower to arpeggiate the notes of the chord.

Be sure to staccato the final two strums in the Intro. In the very next measure, slightly release the tension of your fret-hand fingers to cause the strings to stop ringing between strums. Allow the side of your middle finger to touch the open 3rd string to insure complete silence. In measure 5 of the 1st Verse, use your middle finger to fret the 4th string, your ring finger to fret the 1st, and your pinky to fret the 2nd string on beat 1, and then use your index on the 2nd string for beat 2.

Another style of muted strum is located in measure 4 of the Bridge section. On beat 4, the x's indicate a fret-hand mute. Lay your fingers lightly across the strings so when you strum you don't hear the pitches of the strings. It adds a percussive effect.

This song repeats back to the first page for the 3rd Verse, but it doesn't use repeat signs like some of the other songs. Refer to the *D.S. al Coda* example in the Banjo Notation Legend at the back of the book for a detailed explanation. And like "From Four Until Late," this song has a "fill box."

Love in Vain Blues

This banjo arrangement is based on the "take 1" recording, and is in standard G tuning. If you're playing along with the recording, you'll need to capo at the 1st fret (5th string capoed at the 6th fret).

Me and the Devil Blues

Like "Love in Vain Blues" above, this arrangement is based on the "take 1" recording. From standard G tuning, drop the pitch of the 2nd string a whole step to A. This change takes the open strum from a G major chord to a Gsus2 (suspended 2nd) chord. Next, capo at the 2nd fret. Be sure to capo the 5th string, too.

The staccatoed notes in the first two measures of the 1st Verse are barely audible on Johnson's recording; pick them quietly. At the end of the Verse there's a bit of a finger stretcher in the turnaround. For the triplet on beat 2, begin with your index finger on the 3rd fret of the 4th string, then anchor your pinky at the 5th fret of the 1st string. For the triplet on beat 3, slide your index down a fret and add your middle finger to the 2nd string, 2nd fret. Then for beat 4, slide your index down to the 1st fret while keeping your other fingers planted. If that's too much of a stretch, substitute the open 5th string in place of the notes on the 1st string, 5th fret. For the turnarounds in the subsequent Verses, use your pinky to simultaneously fret the 1st and 2nd strings at the 5th fret. In the 3rd Verse, there are variations that are not written. You might consider omitting the choked 5th and 6th measures and replacing them with the 5th and 6th measures from the 1st Verse.

Ramblin' on My Mind

This arrangement is based on the "take 1" recording, and like "Cross Road Blues," requires a slide. It's in G6 tuning, so from standard G tuning, raise the 1st string up a whole step to E, the 6th note of a G major scale. Then to match the recording, tune each string down a half step.

There's a lot of extra information on each page (w/slide, w/o slide, vibrato, staccato dots, etc.), so take it slow and you'll soon begin to see how it all fits together.

Stop Breakin' Down Blues

This arrangement is also based on the "take 1" recording. To capture the essence of Robert's guitar part, we've used another unusual tuning. Using standard G tuning as your point of reference, tune the 1st string up a whole step to E. Then tune your 2nd string down a whole step to A. From here, the pitches of the remaining strings are lowered substantially. Tune the 3rd and the 5th strings down a minor 3rd to E, and the 4th string down a perfect 4th to A. You'll need to tweak the pitches due to the decreased string tension on the head. Once you're in tune, capo at the 1st fret (capo the 5th string at the 6th fret) to match the recording.

Sweet Home Chicago

This song is in G minor tuning, so if you're already in G tuning, lower the pitch of your 2nd string a half step to B-flat. Then, to play along with the recording, tune all five strings down a half step. The pitch of each of the strings is listed in the tuning legend at the top of the first page of the song.

The song is in a major key, but the minor third note of the G chord is so prevalent that it's necessary to use the minor tuning. Be careful not to pick the 2nd string when it's not called for. In fact, in measure 2 of the Verse, I'd suggest using your middle finger to fret the 2nd string at the 6th fret while barring your index at the 5th fret just in case you pick the string by mistake. It's important to allow the high G note on the 1st string to sustain for the duration of the measure. Then at measure 3 of the Verse, switch to your pinky for the note on the 1st string. Sustained notes on the 1st string are used throughout this song.

In measure 10 of the Verse, use your ring finger to fret the 12th fret of the 1st string, and your middle finger to fret the 12th fret of the 2nd string. Your ring finger will add stability when you choke the 2nd string with your middle finger.

They're Red Hot

From G tuning, raise the pitch of your 1st string a whole step to E.

This is the only song in this banjo collection that is not a shuffle. Keep all your eighth-note strums evenly spaced. Every chord in this song is strummed, so to reduce the clutter on the page, the right-hand fingerings (all "t"s in this case) are included only in measure 1. The *"sim"* label below beat 1 of measure 2 indicates to continue in a similar fashion. Don't let the dots to the right of the tab numbers in measure 6 of the Verse confuse you. They are dotted-quarter notes, and are to be held for 1-1/2 beats each. At the very end of the song, there is a *ritardando*, indicated by the *"rit."* label. Slow the tempo dramatically to add emphasis to the C6 chord strums.

32-20 Blues

This arrangement is in G tuning, and capoed at the 2nd fret (5th string capoed at the 7th). Fret the very first note in the song with your middle finger. This will allow your index and pinky to fret the notes on beat 2.

In measure 1 of the 1st Verse, the notes on beat 1 should be allowed to sustain for the entire measure, so continue to fret the notes of beat 1 while you play the subsequent notes. The same holds true for measures 2 and 3, as well as several other locations of the song.

This song has a lot of verses, so be sure to follow the repeats. Be sure to omit the 2/4 measure in Verses 3 and 5 as indicated by the footnote. Robert inserted a 2/4 bar later in Verse 3, between measures 7 and 8: see Fill 1 at the bottom of the 1st page of the song. Enter back in the main arrangement at the (D7) chord.

Walkin' Blues

This final song is in G tuning and capoed at the 4th fret (5th string capoed at the 9th). This song also employs a slide. Beginning in measure 4 of the Verse, you'll see notes fretted at the 5th fret of the 1st string. They are very quiet, so pick them lightly. Robert also inserted them in the first four measures of subsequent verses.

TUNINGS LIST

Cross Road Blues
(Crossroads)

(take 2)

Words and Music by Robert Johnson

Key of B

G tuning, capo IV:
(5th-1st) G-D-G-B-D

Intro

Moderately slow ♩ = 95

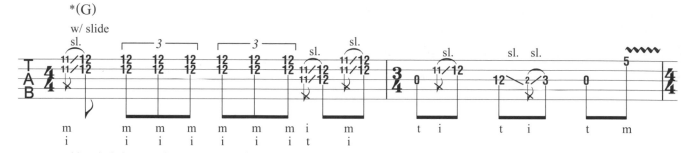

*Symbols in parentheses represent chord names respective to capoed banjo.
Symbols above reflect actual sounding chords. Capoed fret is "0" in tab.

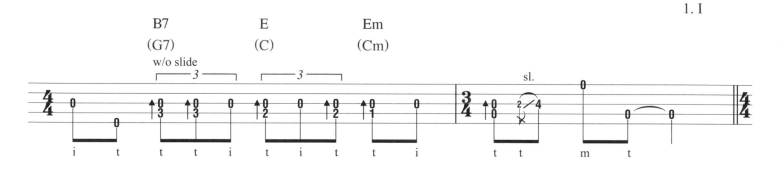

Verse

went to the cross road,   fell down on my knees.

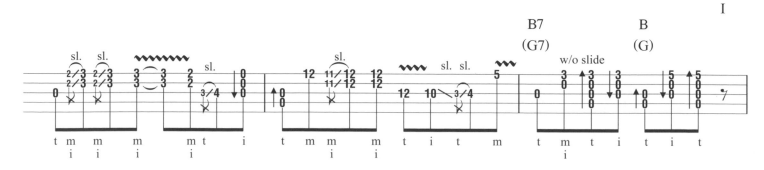

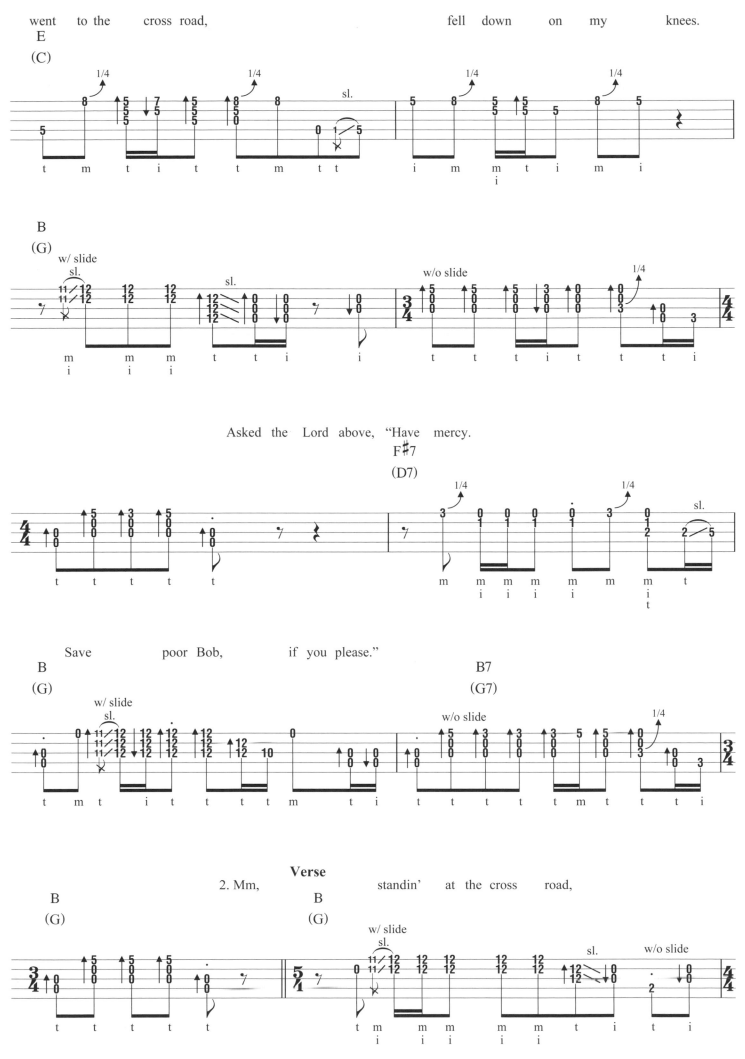

I tried to flag a ride.

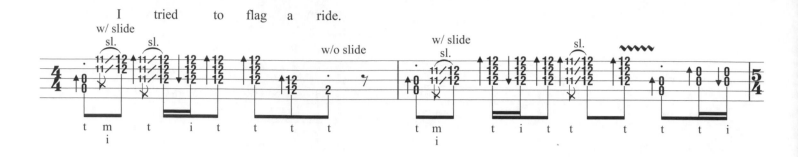

Standin' at the cross

B7

(G7)

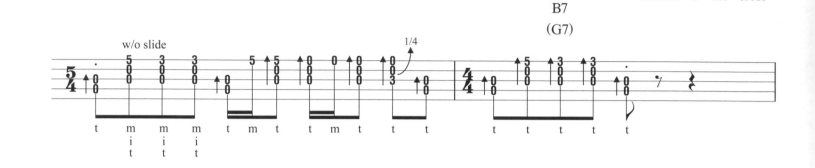

road,

E

(C)

I tried to flag a ride.

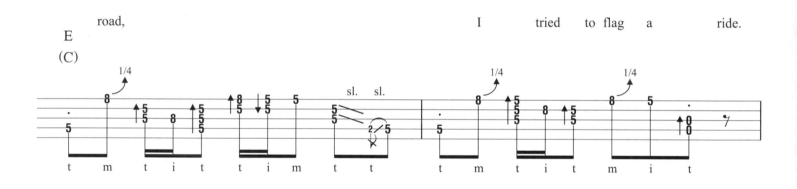

B

(G)

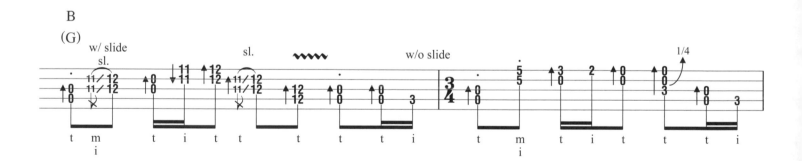

Didn't nobody   seem to know me.   Ev'ry-

F#7

(D7)

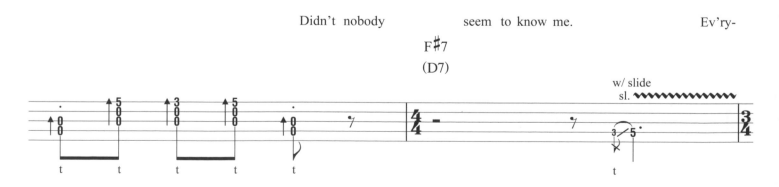

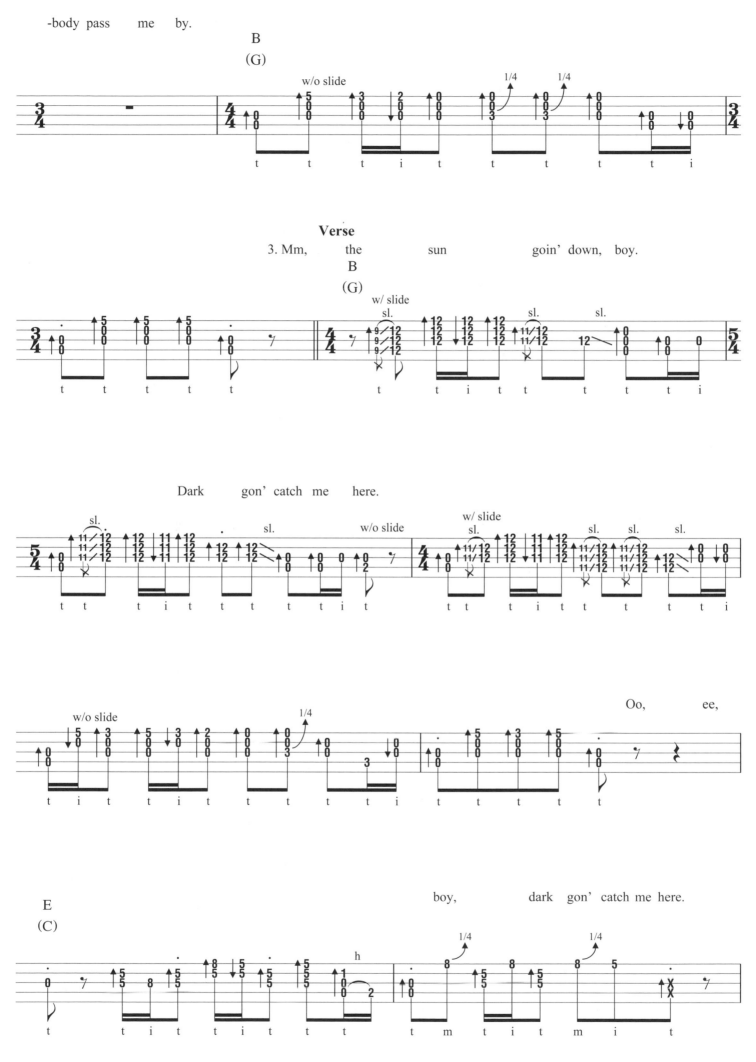

I haven't got no lovin' sweet woman that

love and feel my care.   4. You can

Verse

run,   you can run.   Tell my friend-boy Willie Brown.

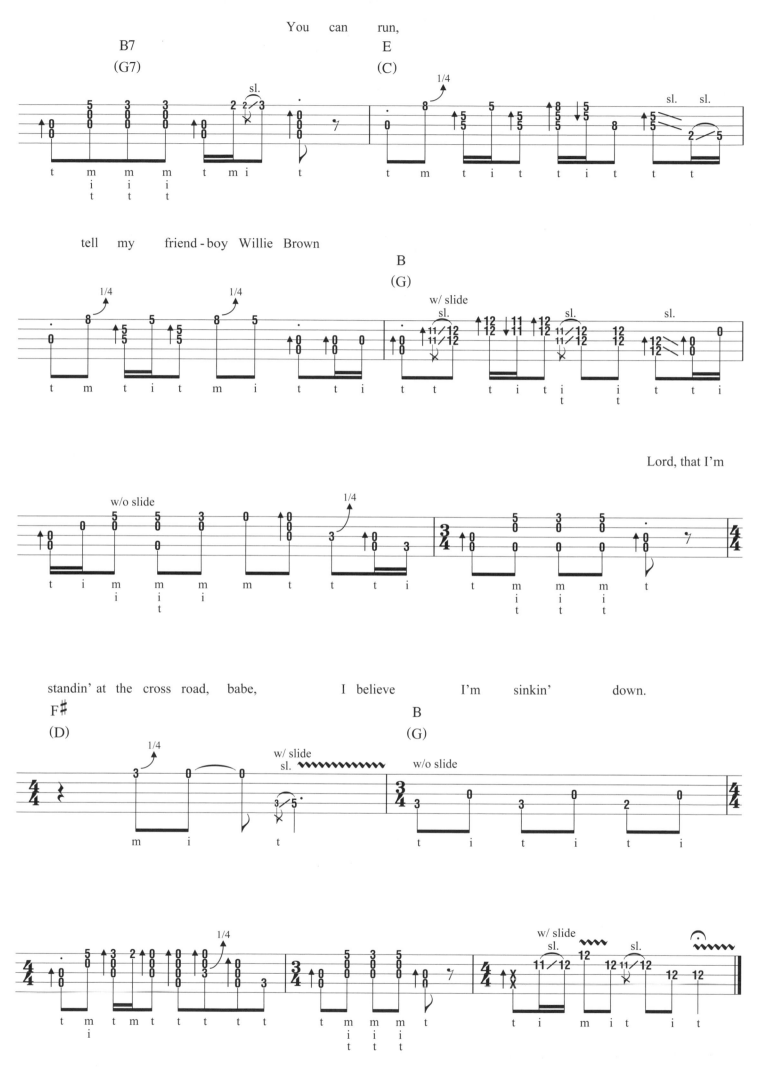

Drunken Hearted Man

(take 1)

Words and Music by Robert Johnson

Key of E♭

Tuning, capo I:
(5th-1st) A-D-G-B-E

Intro

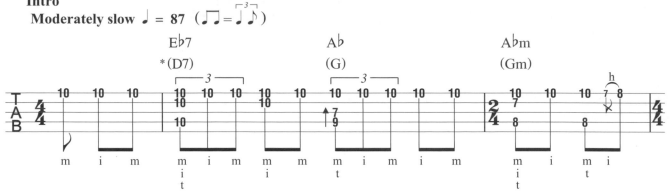

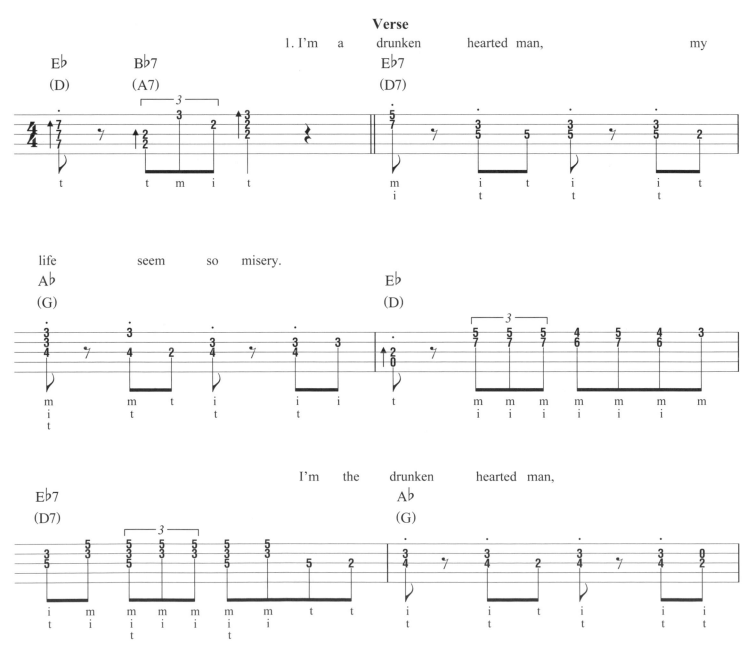

*Symbols in parentheses represent chord names respective to capoed banjo.
Symbols above reflect actual sounding chords. Capoed fret is "0" in tab.

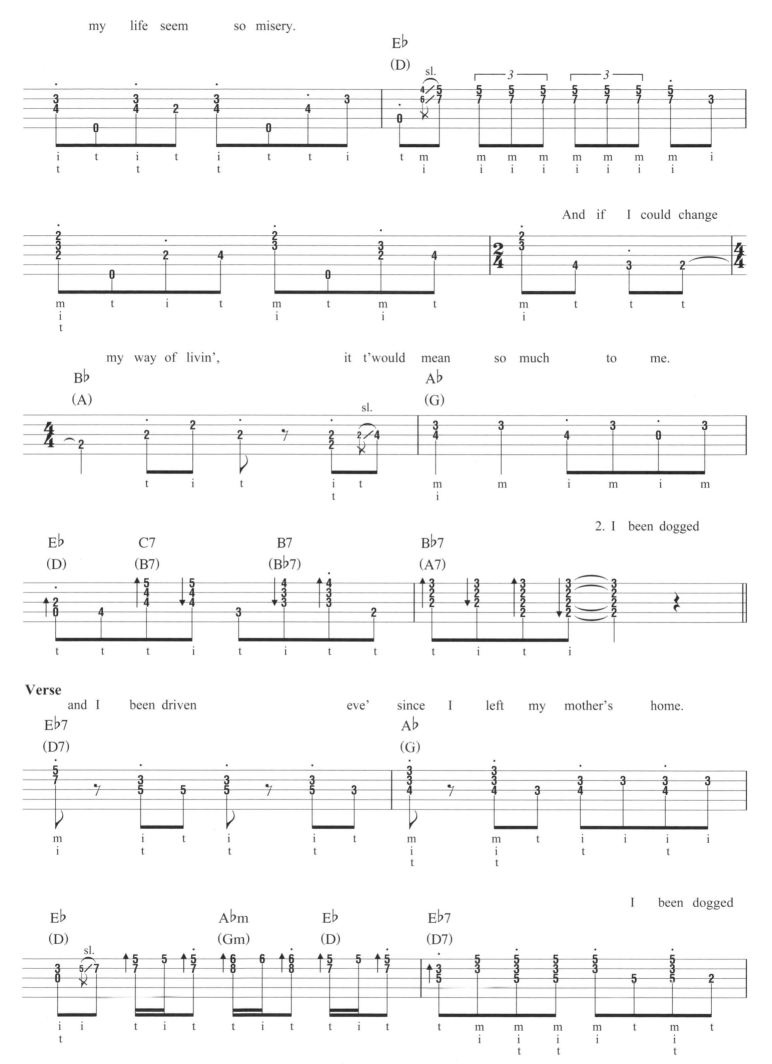

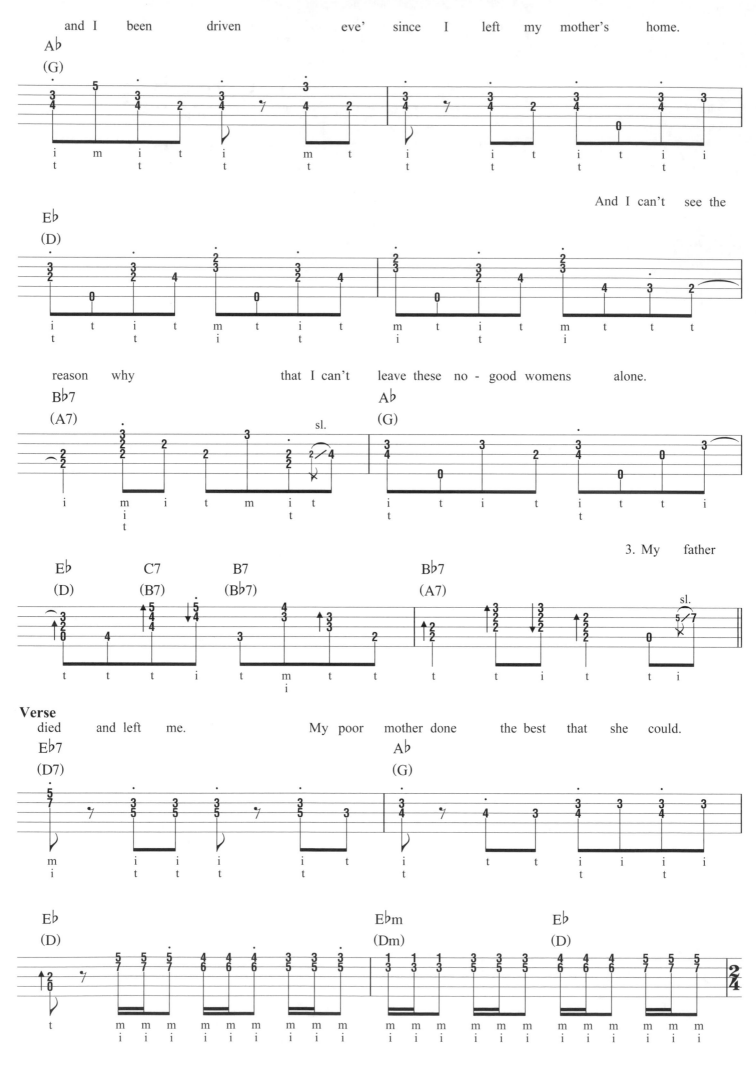

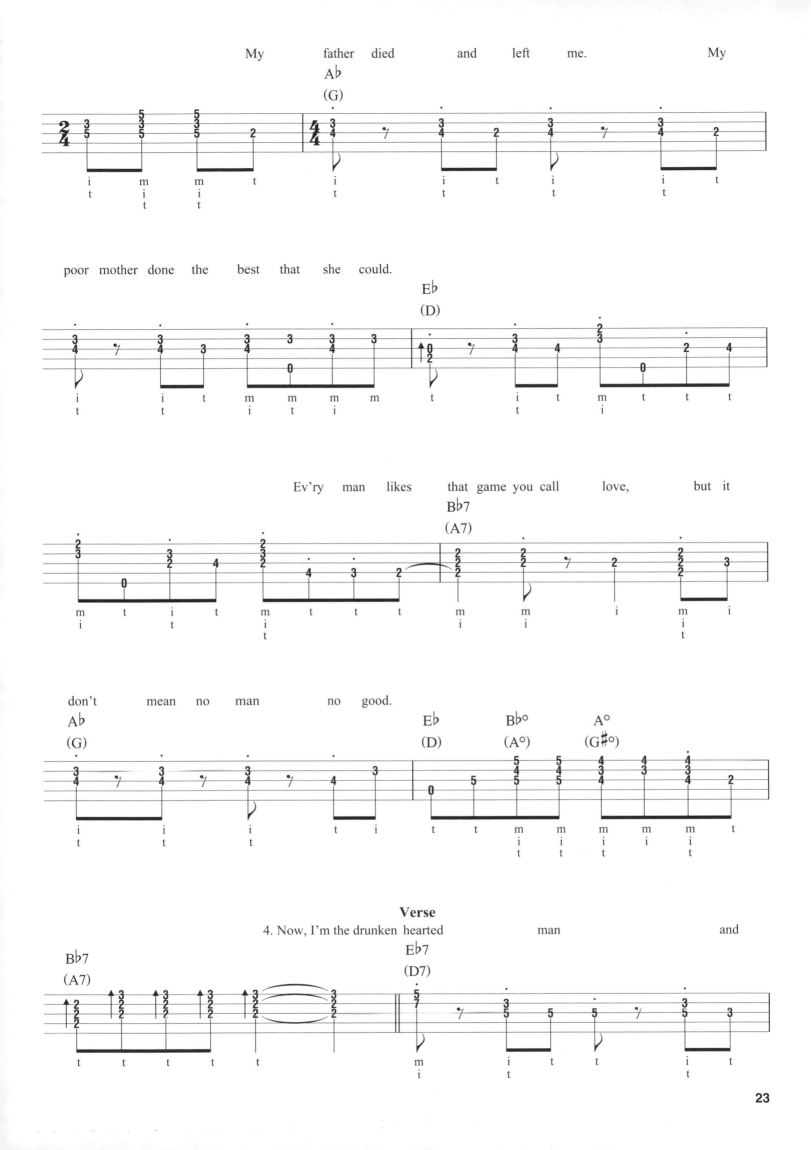

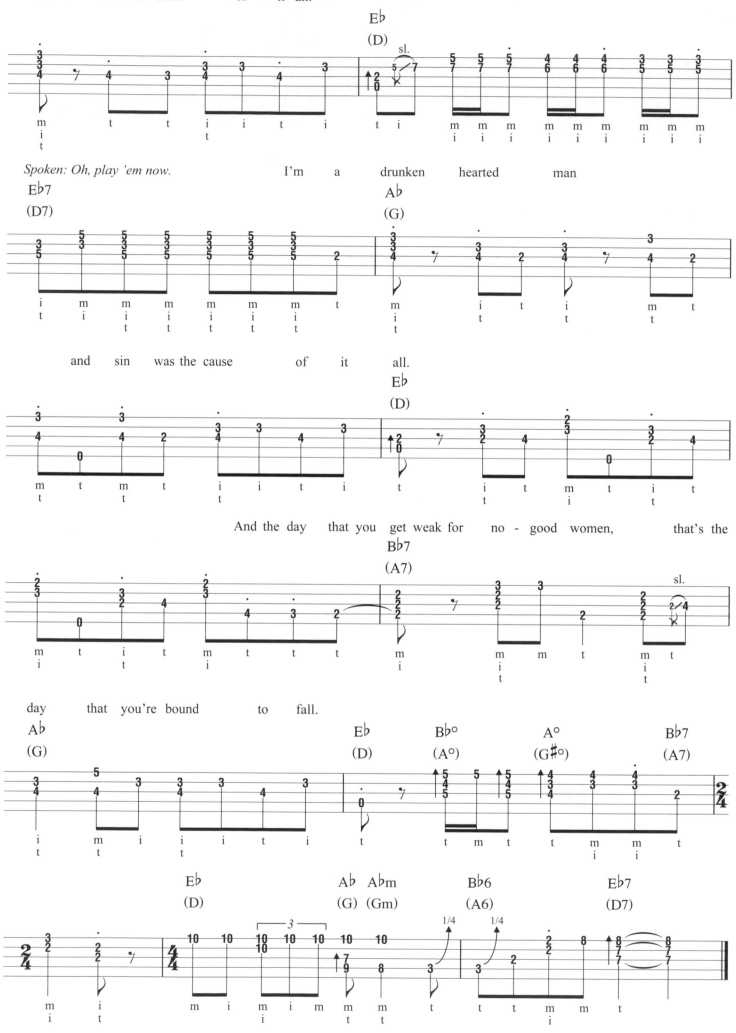

From Four Until Late

Words and Music by Robert Johnson

Key of C

Tuning:
(5th-1st) G-C-G-B-E

Intro
Moderately ♩ = 108

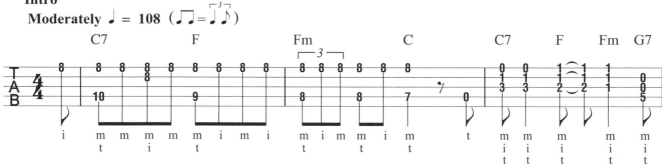

Verse

1. From four un - til late   I was wring - in' my hands   and cryin'.

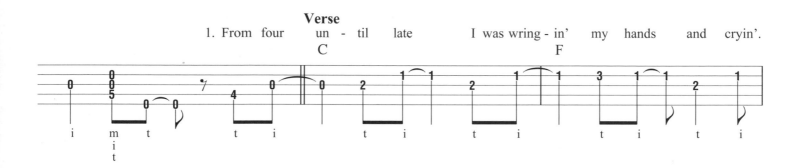

From four   until late   I was wring-

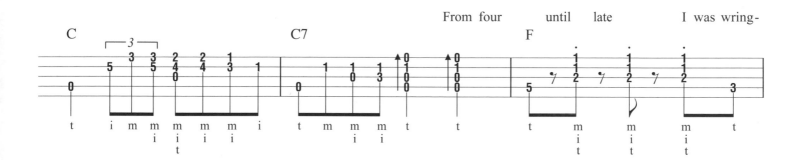

in' my hands   and cryin'.   I believe

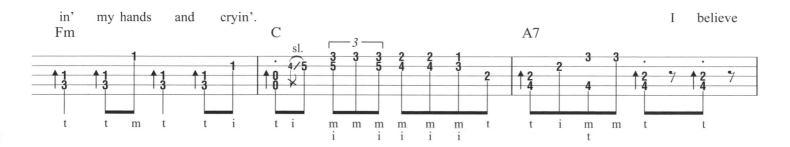

to my soul   that your dad - dy's   Gulf - port bound.

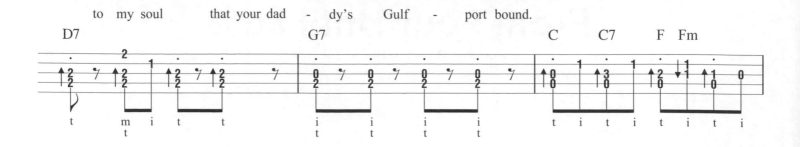

Verse

2. From Memphis   to Norfolk   is a thir - ty - six hours'   ride.

3., 4., 5. *See additional lyrics*

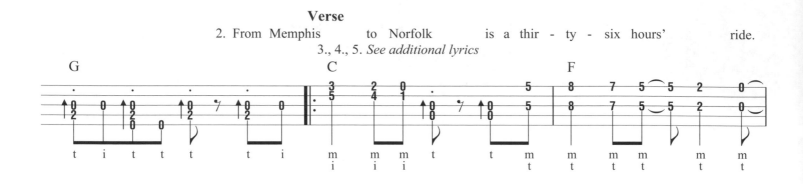

From Memphis   to Norfolk   is a

4th time, w/ Fill 1

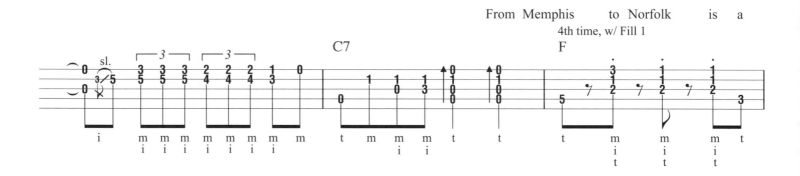

thirty - six hours'   ride.   A man is

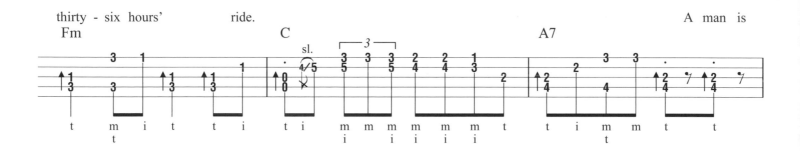

Fill 1

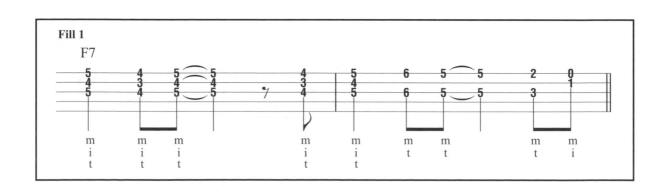

like   a prisoner   and he's nev - er sat - is - fied.

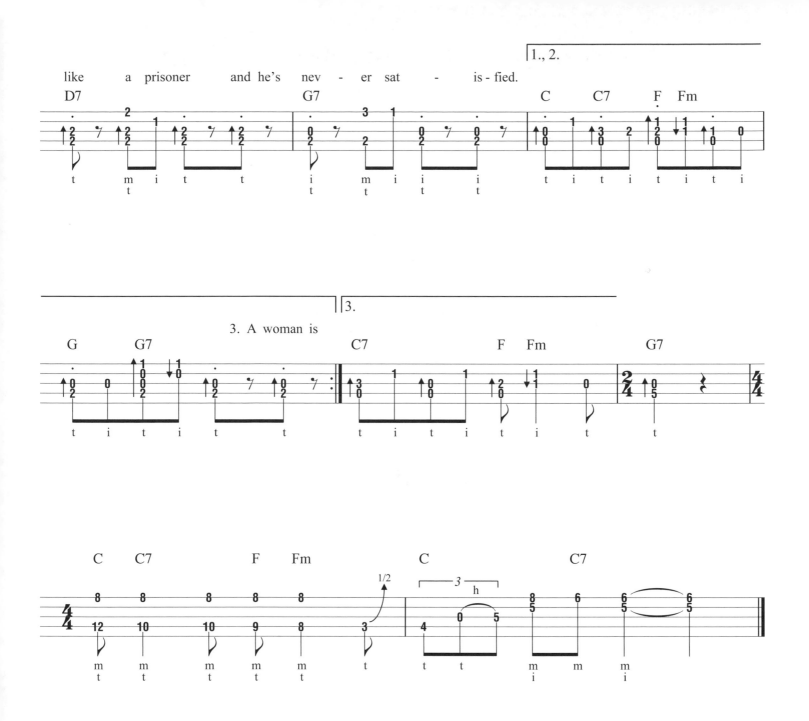

Additional Lyrics

3. A woman is like a dresser,
   Some man always ramblin' through its drawers.
   A woman is like a dresser,
   Some man's always ramblin' through its drawers.
   It cause so many men wear an apron overhall.

4. From four until late,
   She get with a no-good bunch and clown.
   From four until late,
   She get with a no-good bunch and clown.
   Now she won't do nothin'
   But tear a good man' reputation down.

5. When I leave this town,
   I'm 'on' bid you fare, farewell.
   And when I leave this town,
   I'm gon' bid you fare, farewell.
   And when I return again,
   You'll have a great long story to tell.

I Believe I'll Dust My Broom

Words and Music by Robert Johnson

Key of F#

Tuning:
(5th-1st) E-D-A-B-D
Capo II (4th-1st strings)

Intro
Moderately ♩ = 98

1. I'm gon'

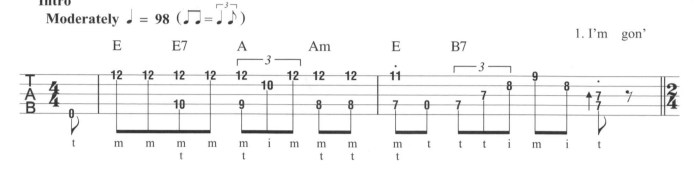

Verse

get up in the morn - in', I be-

2., 3. *See additional lyrics*

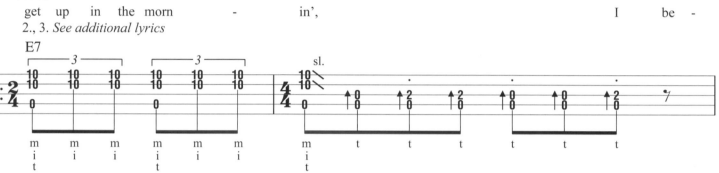

lieve I'll dust my broom. I'm gon'

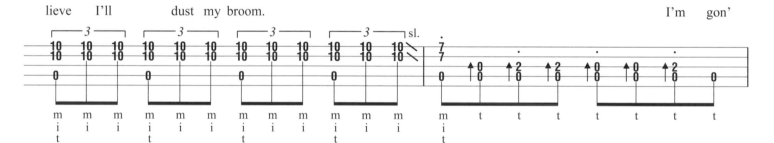

get up in the mornin', I believe I'll dust my broom.

Girlfriend, the black man you been

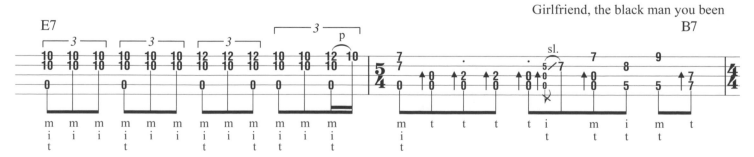

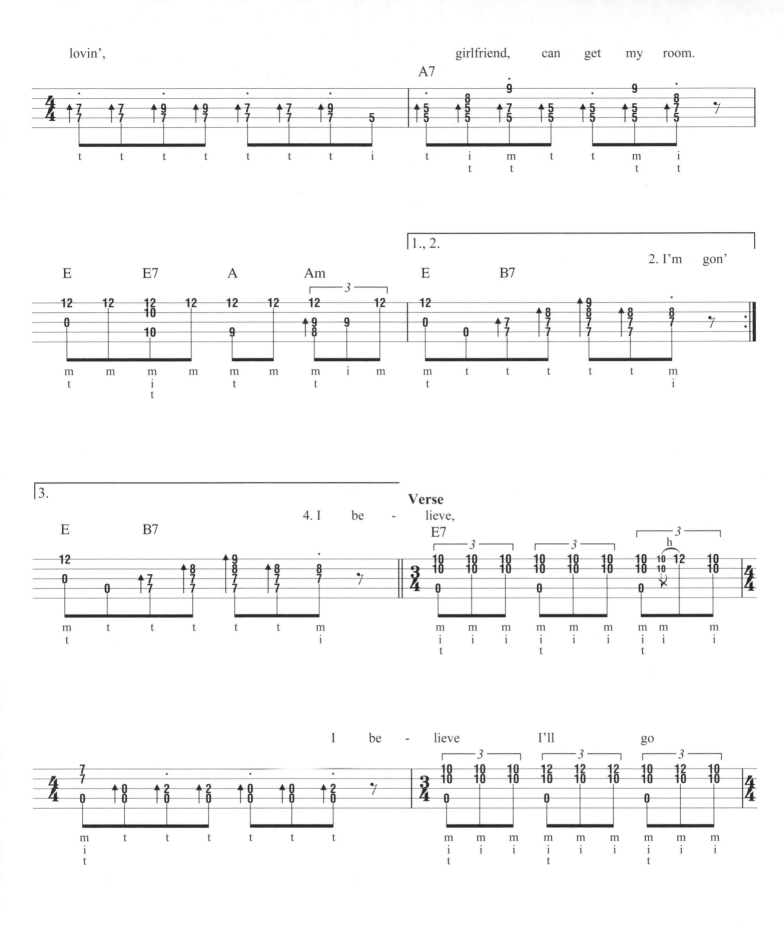

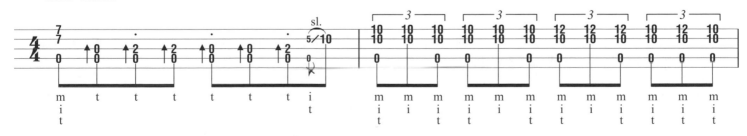

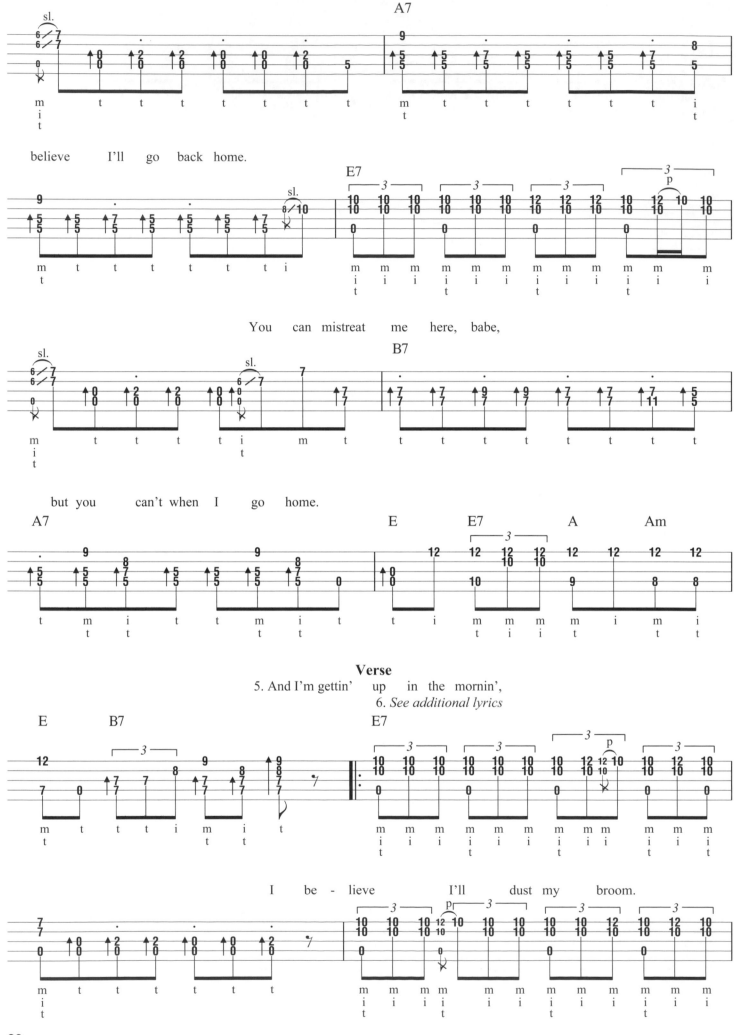

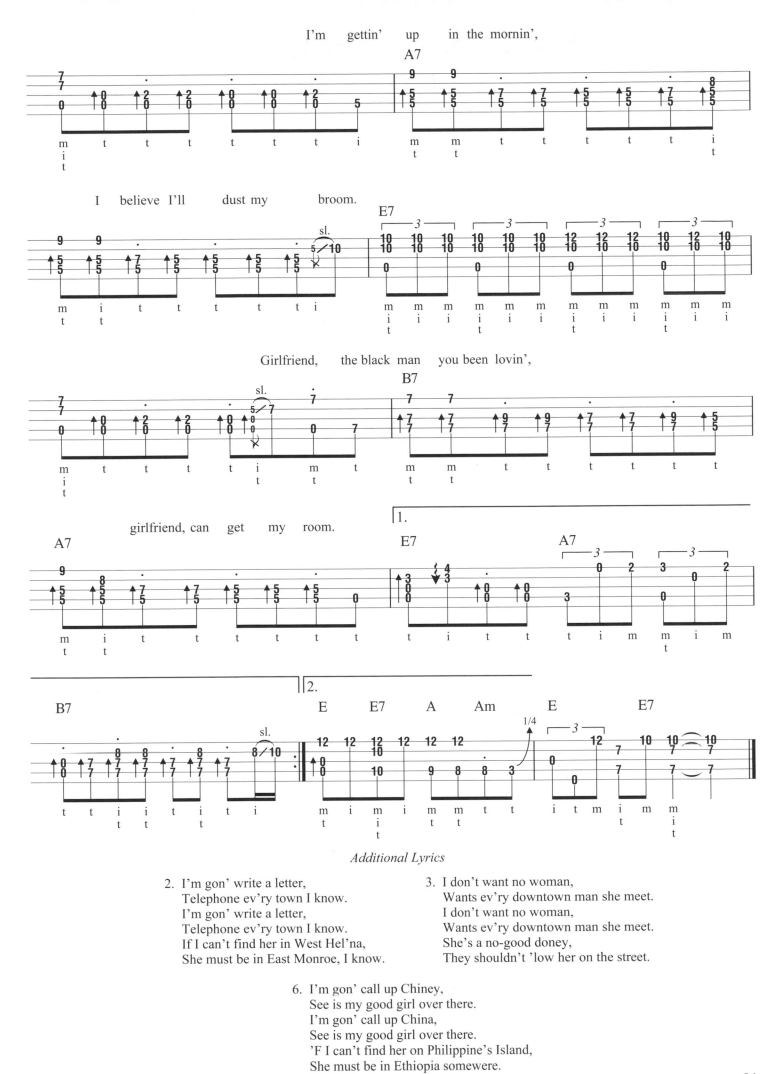

Additional Lyrics

2. I'm gon' write a letter,
   Telephone ev'ry town I know.
   I'm gon' write a letter,
   Telephone ev'ry town I know.
   If I can't find her in West Hel'na,
   She must be in East Monroe, I know.

3. I don't want no woman,
   Wants ev'ry downtown man she meet.
   I don't want no woman,
   Wants ev'ry downtown man she meet.
   She's a no-good doney,
   They shouldn't 'low her on the street.

6. I'm gon' call up Chiney,
   See is my good girl over there.
   I'm gon' call up China,
   See is my good girl over there.
   'F I can't find her on Philippine's Island,
   She must be in Ethiopia somewere.

I'm a Steady Rollin' Man
(Steady Rollin' Man)

Words and Music by Robert Johnson

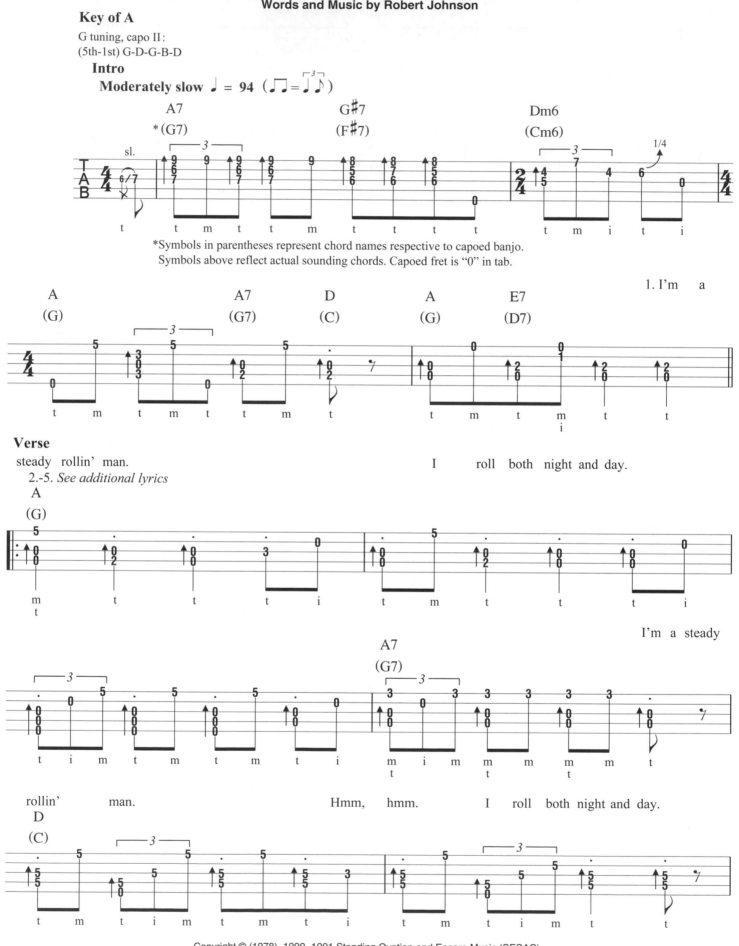

Key of A

G tuning, capo II:
(5th–1st) G-D-G-B-D

Intro

Moderately slow ♩ = 94

*Symbols in parentheses represent chord names respective to capoed banjo.
Symbols above reflect actual sounding chords. Capoed fret is "0" in tab.

1. I'm a

Verse

steady rollin' man.

2.-5. See additional lyrics

I roll both night and day.

I'm a steady

rollin' man.   Hmm, hmm.   I roll both night and day.

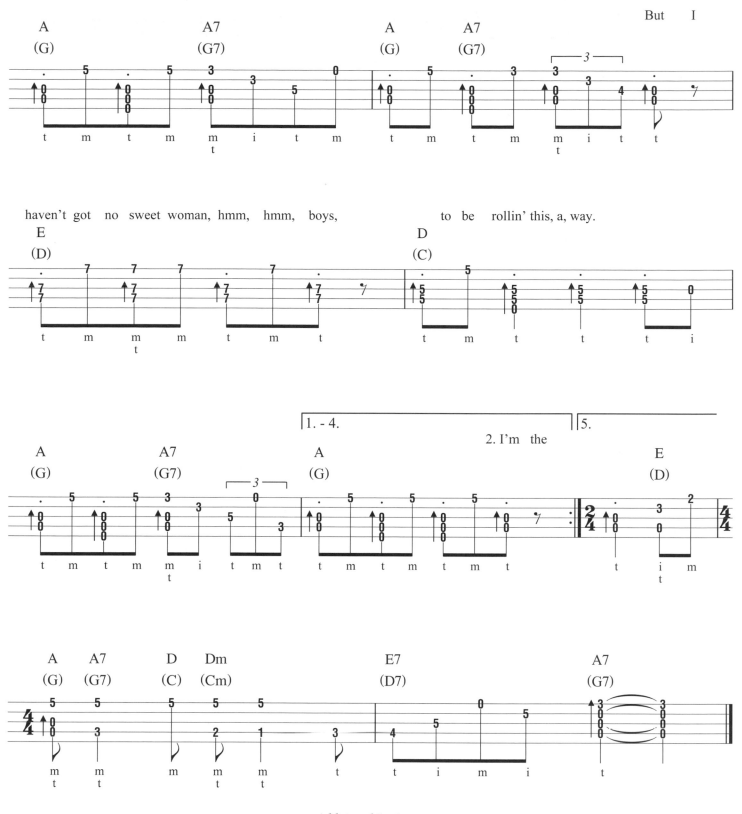

haven't got no sweet woman, hmm, hmm, boys, to be rollin' this, a, way.

Additional Lyrics

2. I'm the man that rolls
   When icicles is hangin' on the tree.
   I'm the man that roll
   When icicles is hangin' on the tree.
   And now you hear me howlin', baby, hmm,
   Down on my bended knee.

3. I'm a hard workin' man,
   Have been for many years, I know.
   I'm a hard workin' man,
   Have been for many years, I know.
   And some cream puff's usin' my money, ooh,
   Well, babe, but that'll never be no more.

4. You can't give your sweet woman
   Everything she wants in one time.
   Ooh, hoo, ooo, you can't give your sweet woman
   Everything she wants in one time.
   Well boys, she get ramblin' in her brain, hmm,
   Some monkey man on her mind.

5. I'm a steady rollin' man,
   I roll both night and day.
   I'm a steady rollin' man,
   And I roll both night and day.
   Well I don't have no sweet woman, hmm, boys
   To be rollin' this, a, way.

Kind Hearted Woman Blues

(take 1)

Words and Music by Robert Johnson

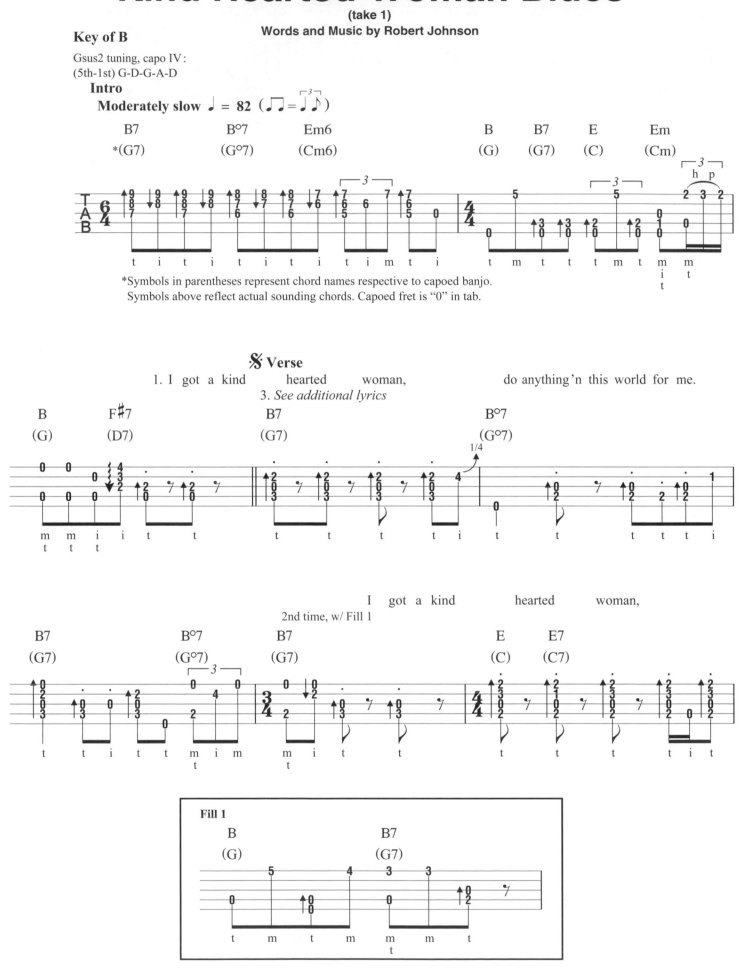

*Symbols in parentheses represent chord names respective to capoed banjo.
Symbols above reflect actual sounding chords. Capoed fret is "0" in tab.

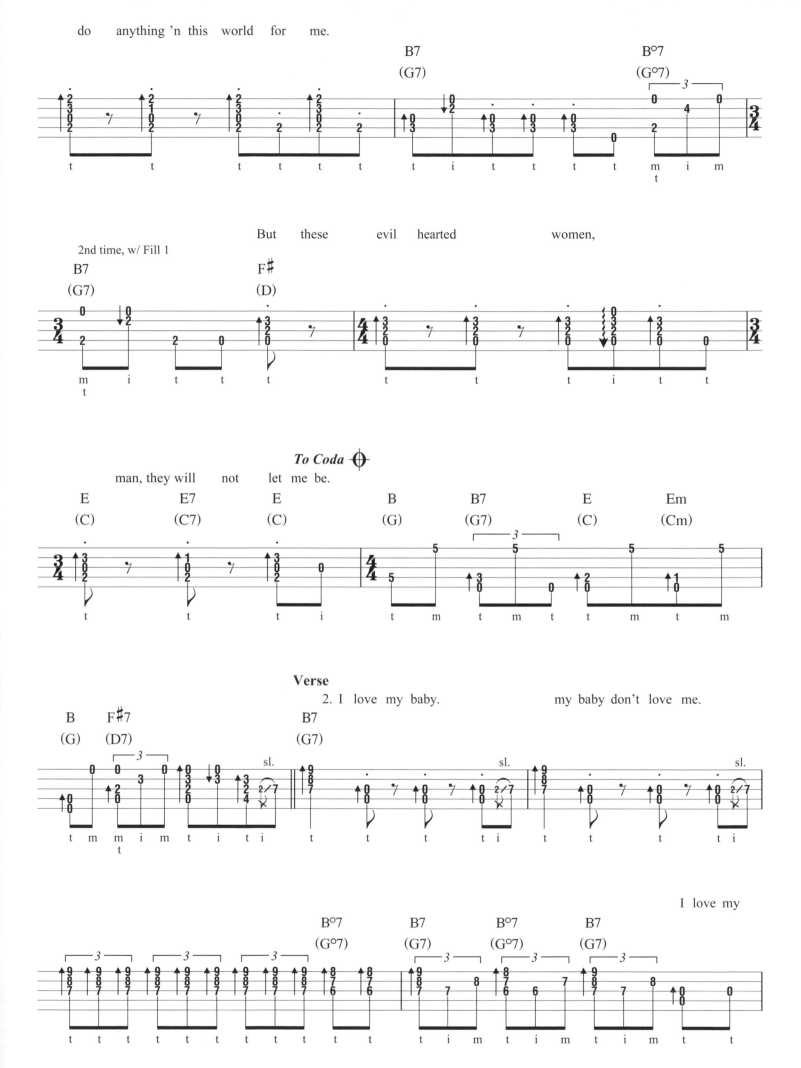

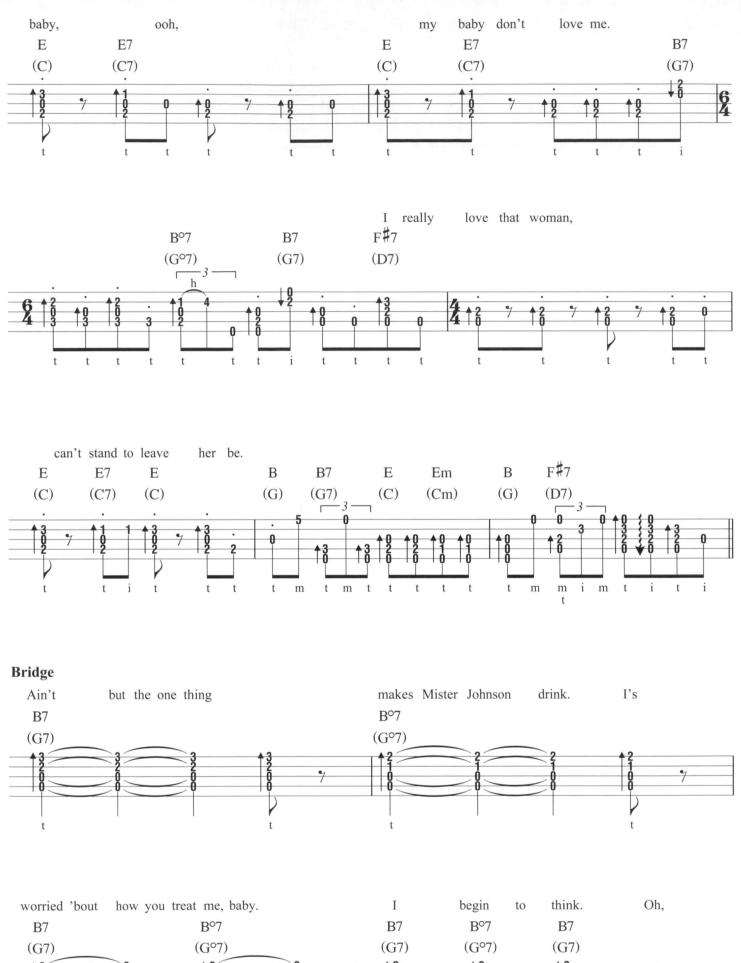

Bridge

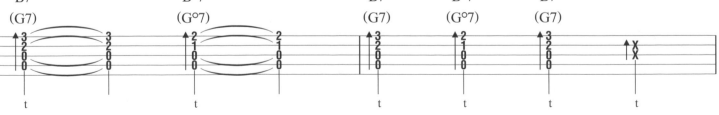

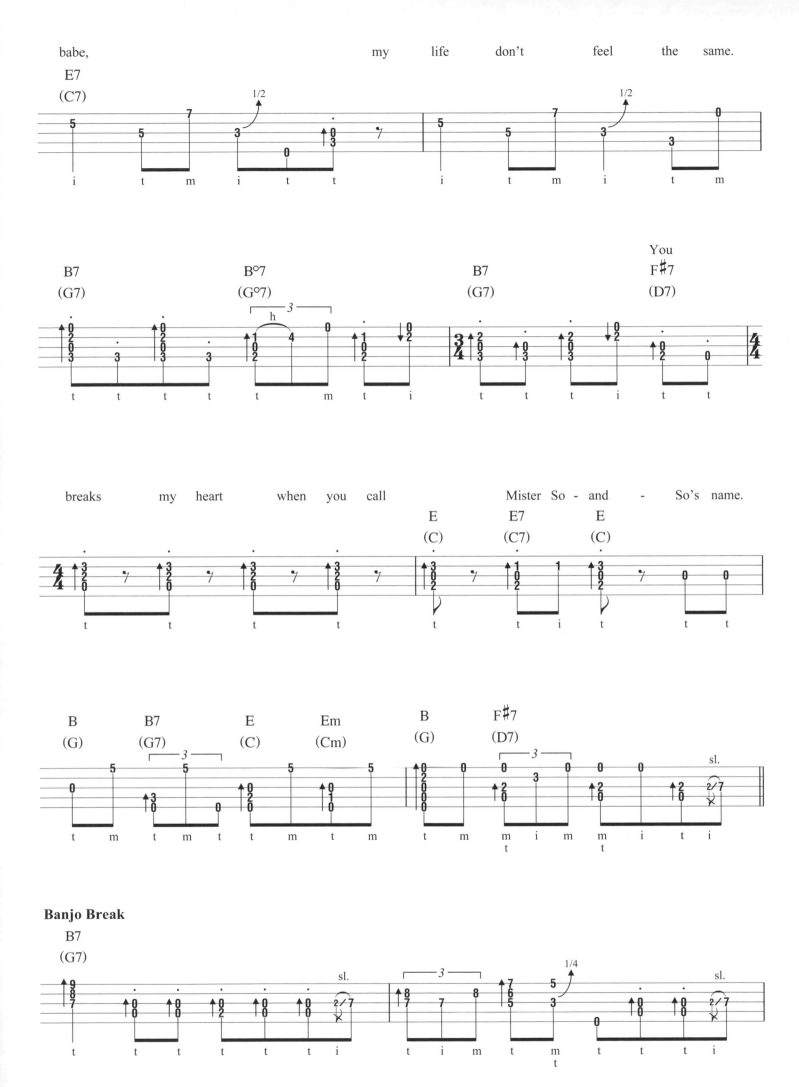

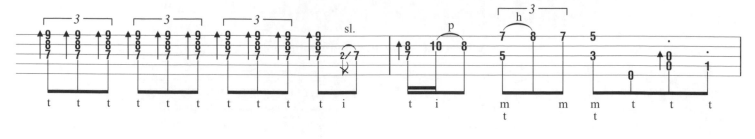

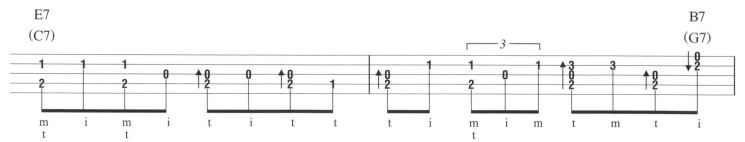

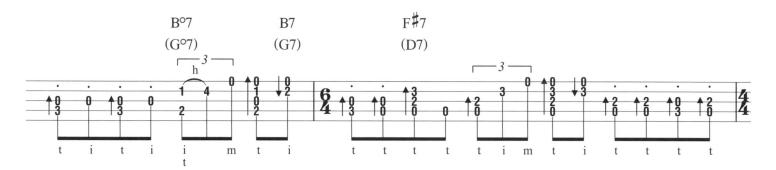

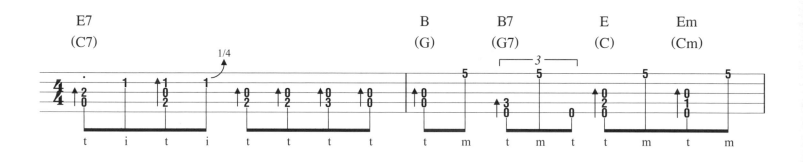

D.S. al Coda

3. She's a kind

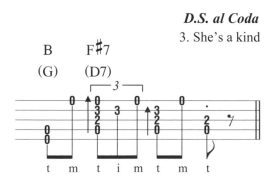

⊕ **Coda**

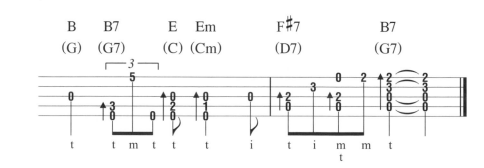

Additional Lyrics

3. She's a kind hearted woman,
   She studies evil all the time.
   She's a kind hearted woman,
   She studies evil all the time.
   You well's to kill me,
   As to have it on your mind.

Hell Hound on My Trail

Words and Music by Robert Johnson

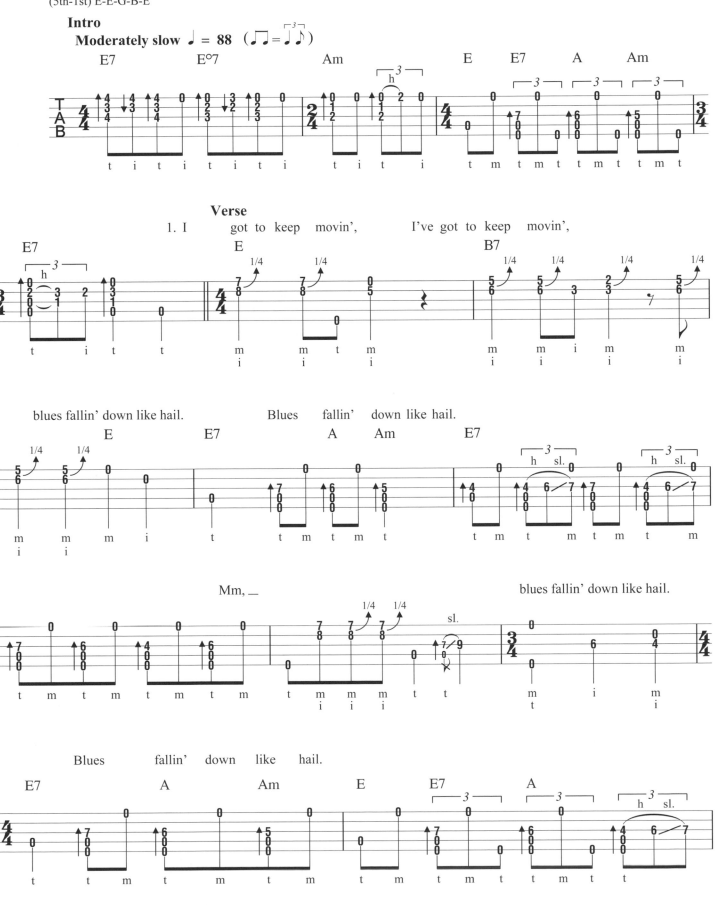

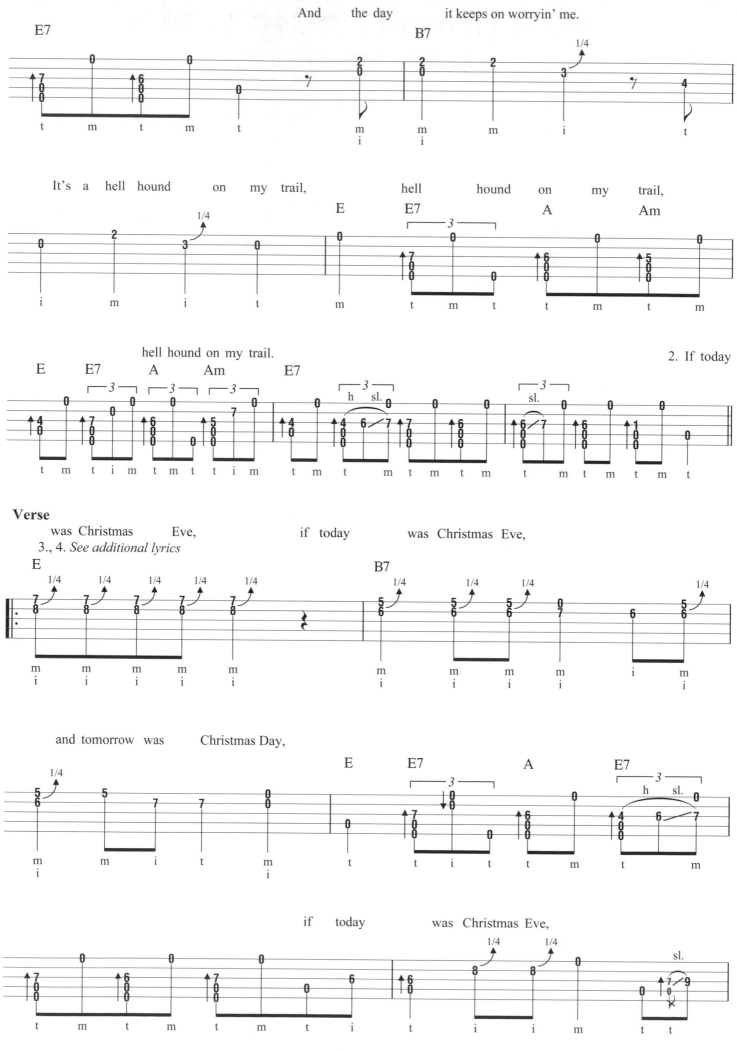

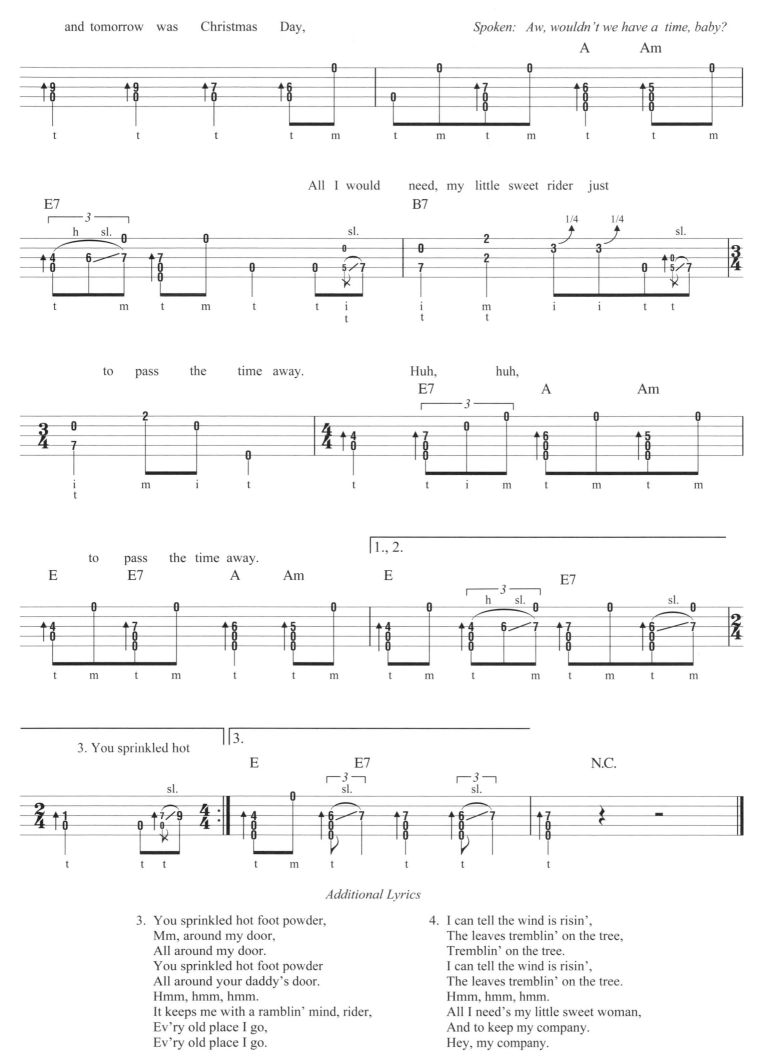

Additional Lyrics

3. You sprinkled hot foot powder,
   Mm, around my door,
   All around my door.
   You sprinkled hot foot powder
   All around your daddy's door.
   Hmm, hmm, hmm.
   It keeps me with a ramblin' mind, rider,
   Ev'ry old place I go,
   Ev'ry old place I go.

4. I can tell the wind is risin',
   The leaves tremblin' on the tree,
   Tremblin' on the tree.
   I can tell the wind is risin',
   The leaves tremblin' on the tree.
   Hmm, hmm, hmm.
   All I need's my little sweet woman,
   And to keep my company.
   Hey, my company.

Love in Vain Blues

(take 1)

Words and Music by Robert Johnson

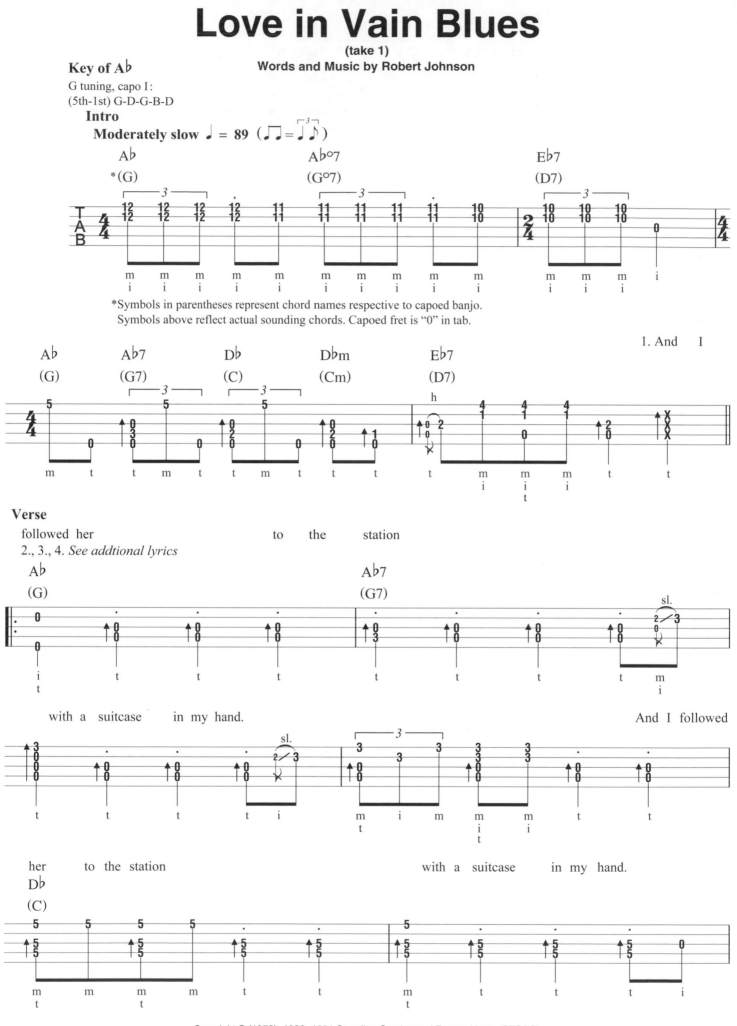

*Symbols in parentheses represent chord names respective to capoed banjo.
Symbols above reflect actual sounding chords. Capoed fret is "0" in tab.

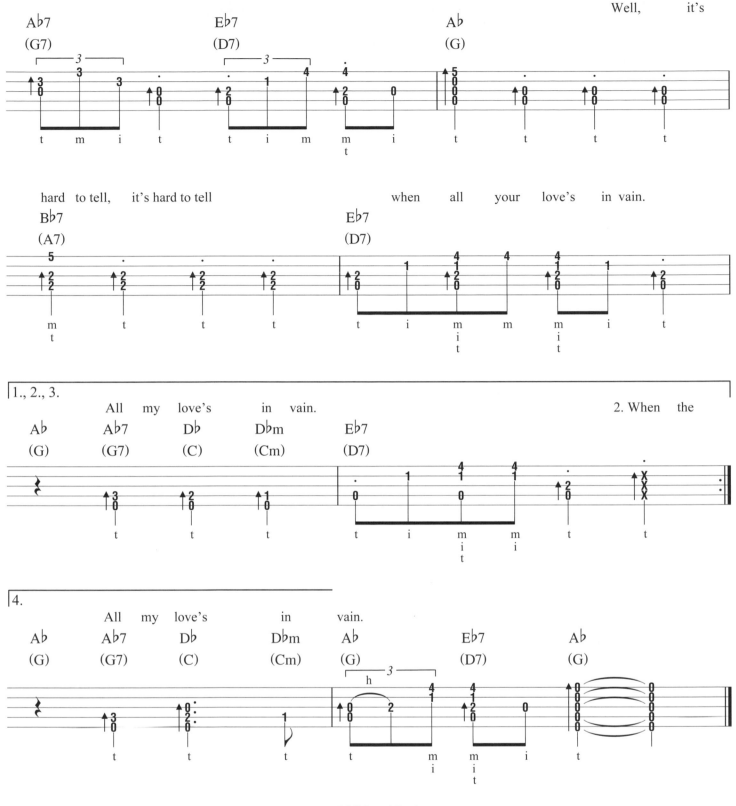

Additional Lyrics

2. When the train rolled up to the station,
   I looked her in the eye.
   When the train rolled up to the station,
   And I looked her in the eye.
   Well, I was lonesome, I felt so lonesome
   And I could not help but cry.
   All my love's in vain.

3. When the train, it left the station
   With two lights on behind.
   When the train, it left the station
   With two lights on behind.
   Well, the blue light was my blues
   And the red light was my mind.
   All my love's in vain.

4. Ou, hou, hoo, Willie Mae.
   Oh, oh, hey, Willie Mae.
   Ou, ou, ou, ou,
   Hee, vee, oh, woe.
   All my love's in vain.

Me and the Devil Blues

(take 1)
Words and Music by Robert Johnson

Key of B♭

Gsus2 tuning, capo III:
(5th-1st) G-D-G-A-D

Intro

Moderately slow ♩ = 85

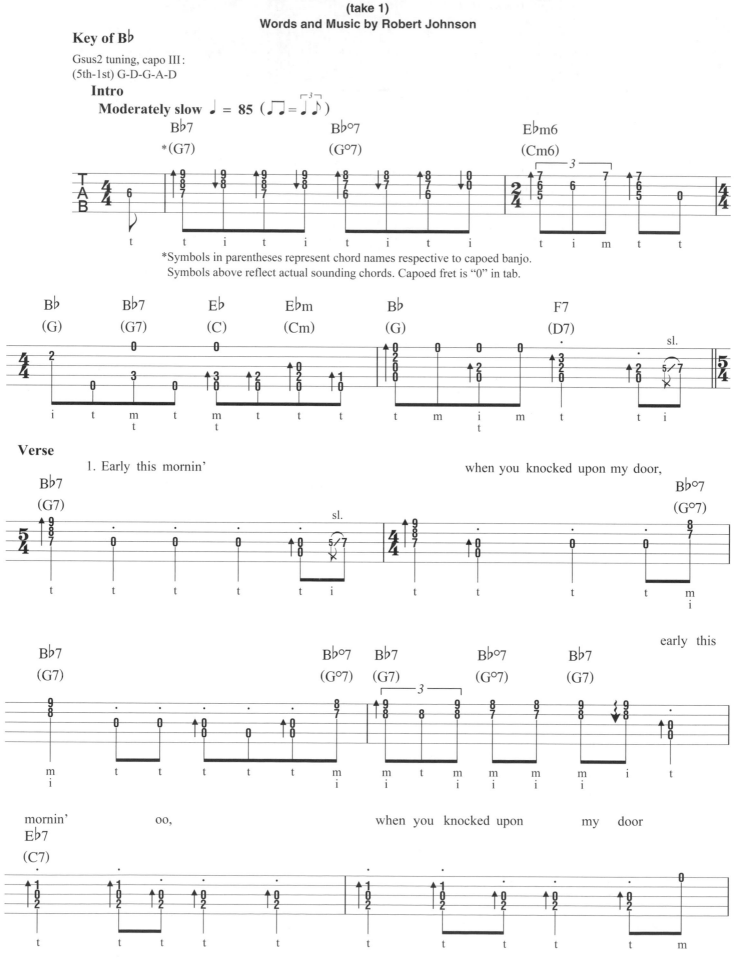

*Symbols in parentheses represent chord names respective to capoed banjo.
Symbols above reflect actual sounding chords. Capoed fret is "0" in tab.

Verse

1. Early this mornin'   when you knocked upon my door,

early this

mornin'   oo,   when you knocked upon   my door

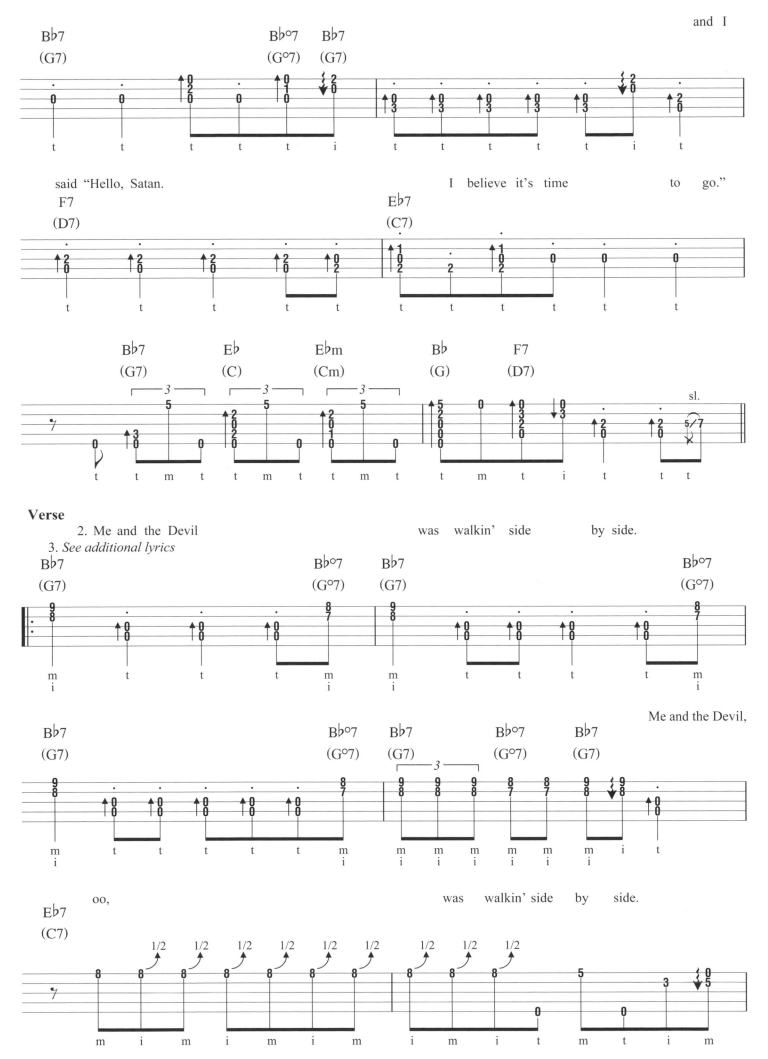

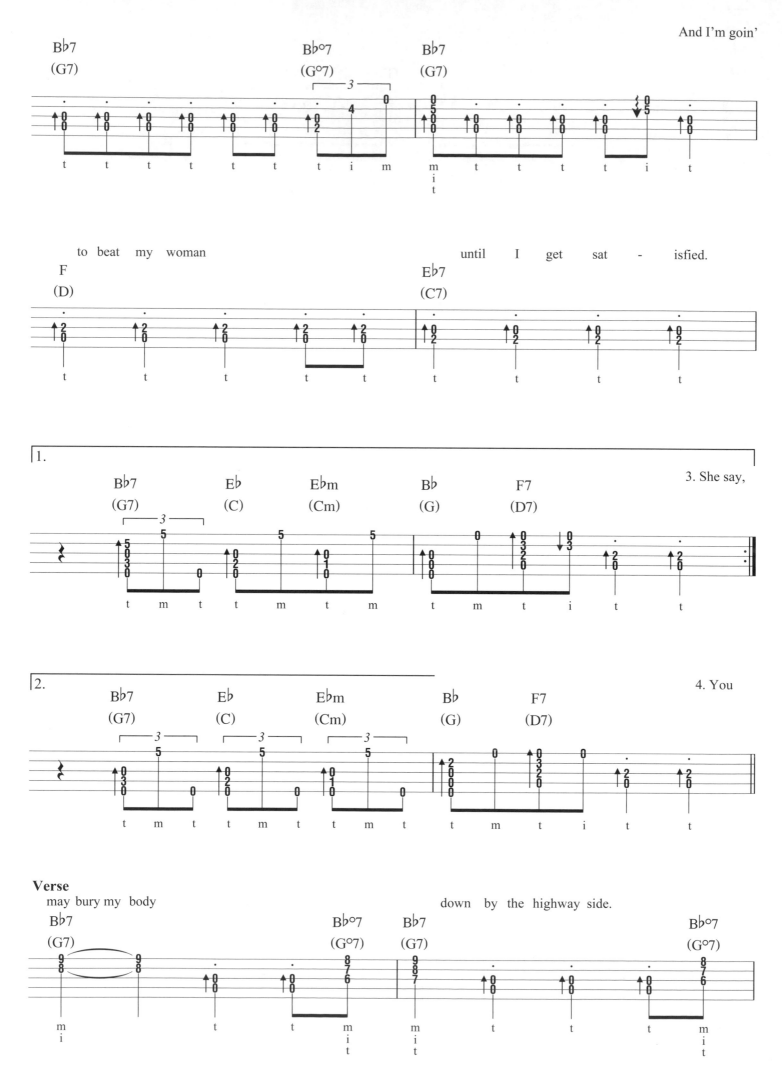

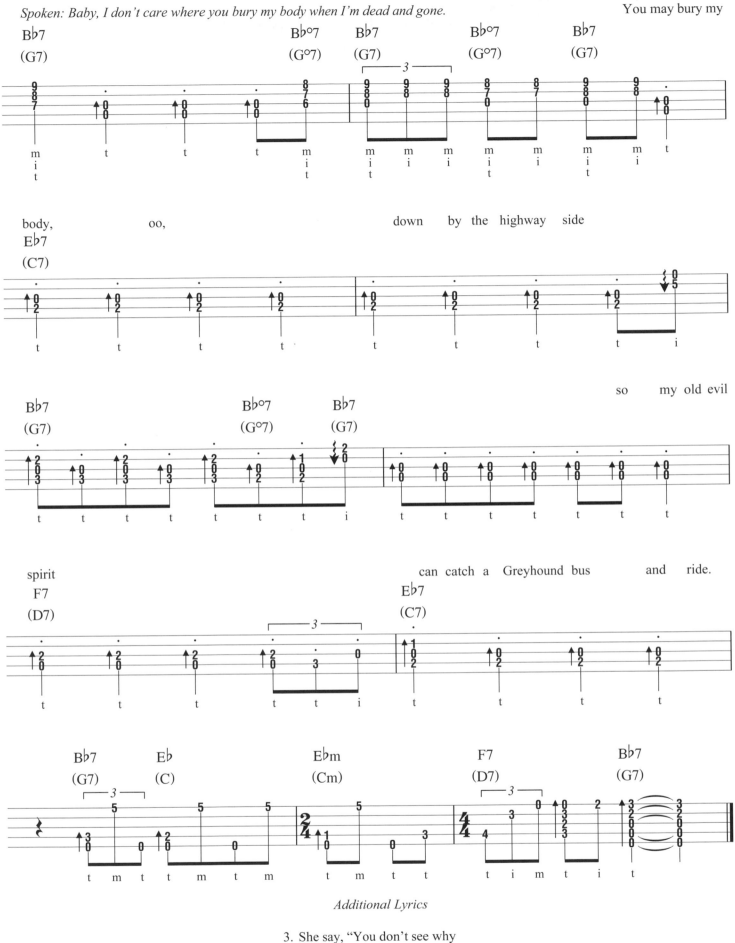

Additional Lyrics

3. She say, "You don't see why
   That you will dog me 'round."
   Now babe, you know you ain't doin' me right, don' cha?
   She say, "You don't see why, oo,
   That you will dog me 'round."
   It must-a be that old evil spirit
   So deep down in the ground.

Stop Breakin' Down Blues

(take 1)

Words and Music by Robert Johnson

Key of Bb

A5 tuning, capo I:
(5th-1st) E-A-E-A-E

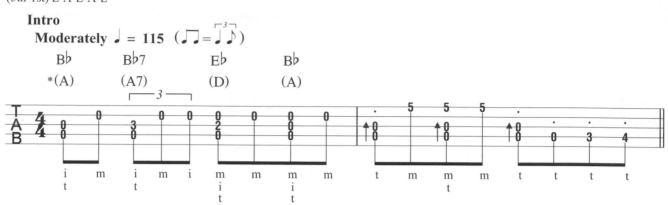

*Symbols in parentheses represent chord names respective to capoed banjo.
Symbols above reflect actual sounding chords. Capoed fret is "0" in tab.

Verse

1. Ev - 'ry - time I'm walkin' down the streets,
2.-5. *See additional lyrics*

some pretty mama start breakin' down with me. Stop breakin'

down. Yes, stop breakin' down.

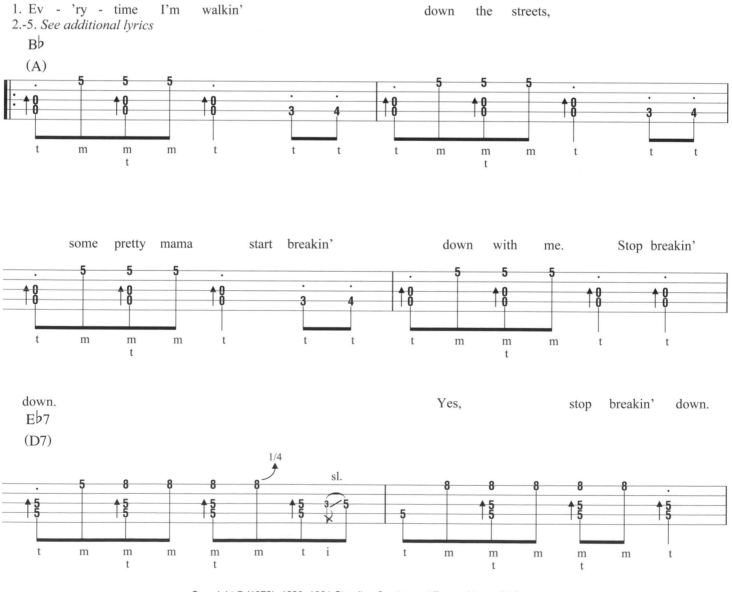

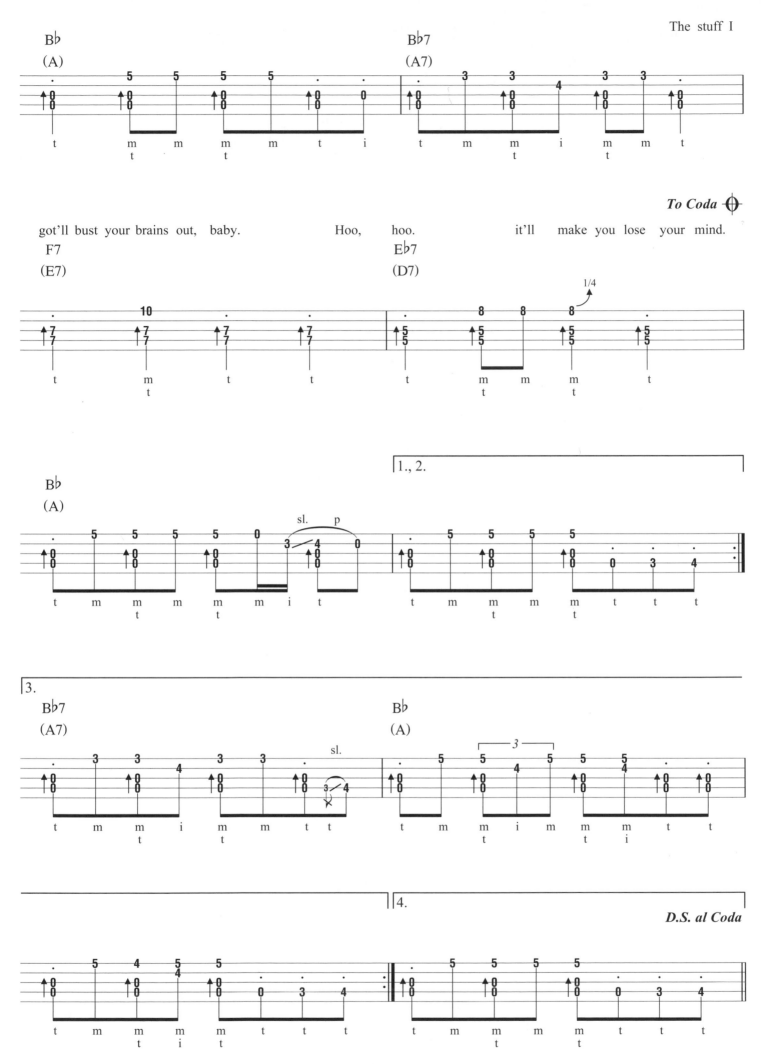

got'll bust your brains out, baby.   Hoo,   hoo.   it'll   make you lose   your mind.

Coda

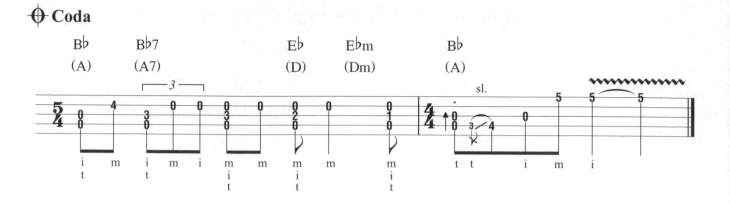

Additional Lyrics

2. I can't walk the streets, now,
    Con, consulate my mind.
    Some no good woman,
    She starts breakin' down.
    Stop breakin' down,
    Please, stop breakin' down.
    The stuff I got, it gon' bust your brains out.
    Hoo, hoo, it'll make you lose your mind.

3. Now, you Saturday night womens,
    You love to ape and clown.
    You won't do nothin'
    But tear a good man reputation down.
    Stop breakin' down,
    Please, stop breakin' down.
    The stuff I got'll bust your brains out, baby.
    Hoo, hoo, it'll make you lose your mind.

4. Now, I give my baby, now,
    The ninty-nine degree.
    She jumped up
    And throwed a pistol down on me.
    Stop breakin' down,
    Please, stop breakin' down.
    Stuff I got'll bust your brains out, baby.
    Hoo, hoo, it'll make you lose your mind.

5. I can't start walkin'
    Down the streets.
    But some pretty mamma
    Don't start breakin' down with me.
    Stop breakin' down,
    Yes, stop breakin' down.
    The stuff I got'll bust your brains out, baby.
    Hoo, hoo, it'll make you lose your mind.

Sweet Home Chicago

Words and Music by Robert Johnson

Key of F#

Gm tuning, down 1/2 step:
(5th-1st) F#-C#-F#-A-C#

Intro

Moderately slow ♩ = 94

1. Oh,

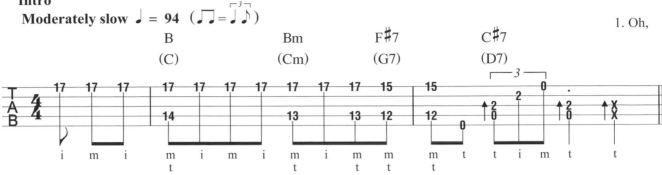

Verse

baby, don't you want to go?

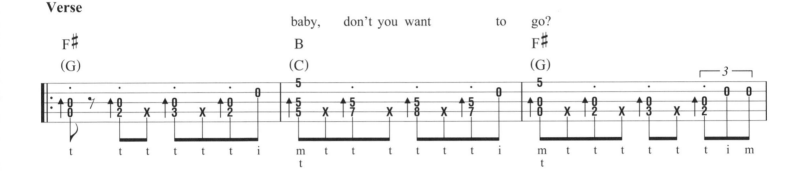

Oh, baby, don't you want to

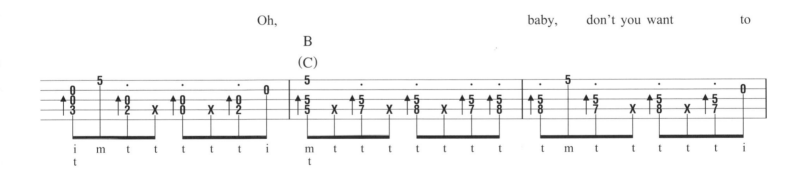

go back to the land of California to my

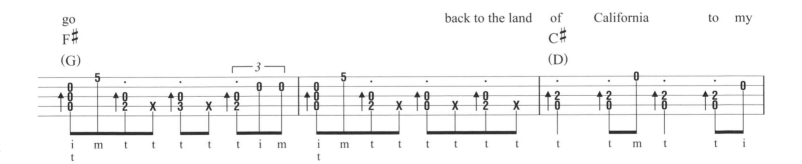

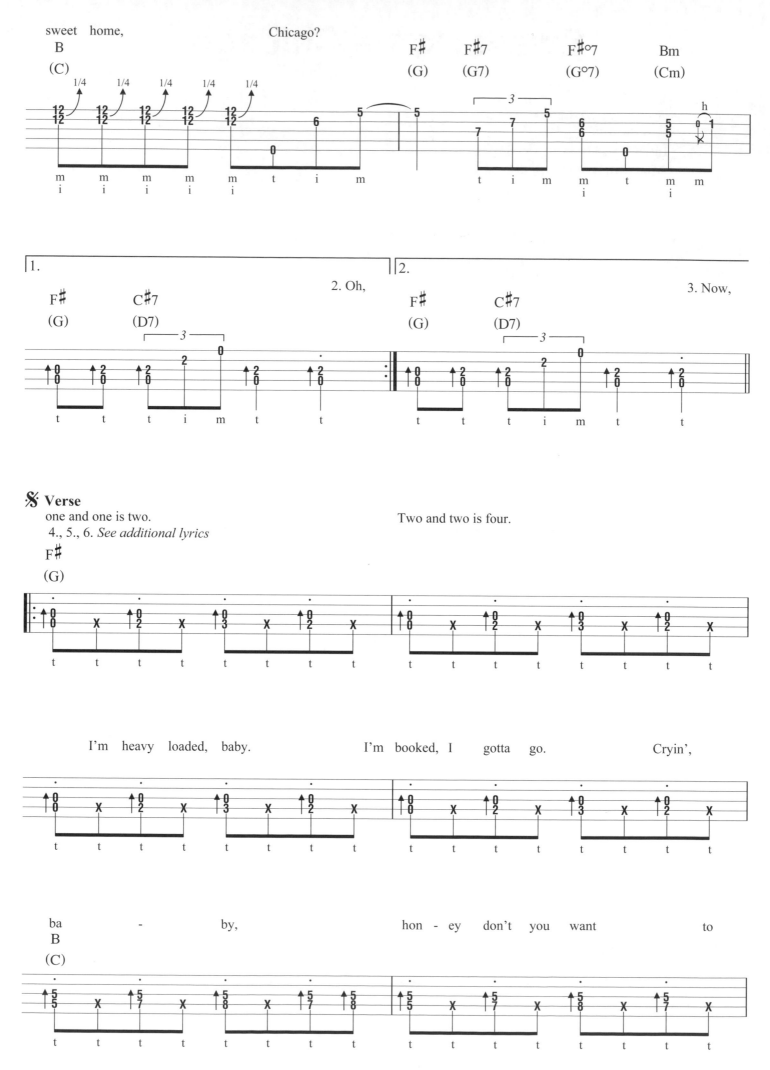

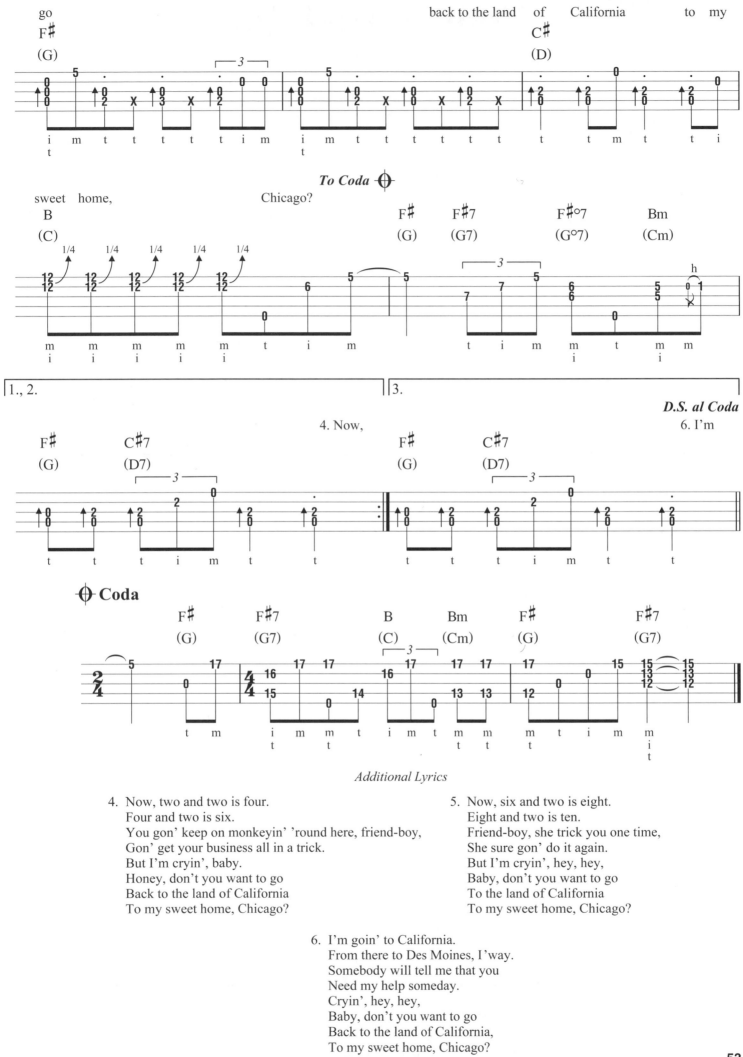

Additional Lyrics

4. Now, two and two is four.
   Four and two is six.
   You gon' keep on monkeyin' 'round here, friend-boy,
   Gon' get your business all in a trick.
   But I'm cryin', baby.
   Honey, don't you want to go
   Back to the land of California
   To my sweet home, Chicago?

5. Now, six and two is eight.
   Eight and two is ten.
   Friend-boy, she trick you one time,
   She sure gon' do it again.
   But I'm cryin', hey, hey,
   Baby, don't you want to go
   To the land of California
   To my sweet home, Chicago?

6. I'm goin' to California.
   From there to Des Moines, I'way.
   Somebody will tell me that you
   Need my help someday.
   Cryin', hey, hey,
   Baby, don't you want to go
   Back to the land of California,
   To my sweet home, Chicago?

They're Red Hot

Words and Music by Robert Johnson

Key of G

G6 tuning:
(5th-1st) G-D-G-B-E

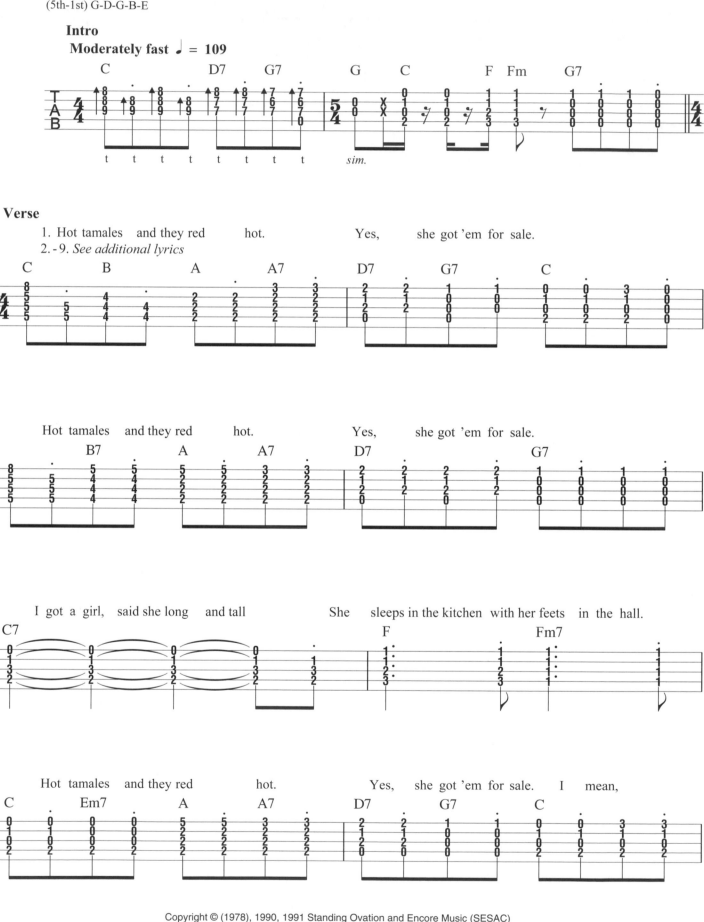

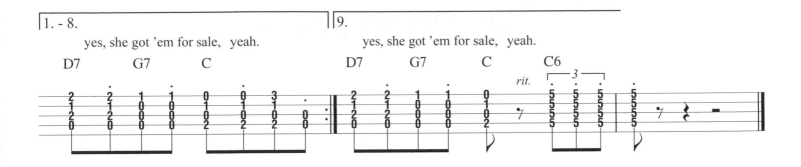

Additional Lyrics

2. Hot tamales and they red hot.
   Yes, she got 'em for sale.
   Hot tamales and they red hot.
   Yes, she got 'em for sale.
   She got two for a nickel, got four for a dime.
   Would sell you more,
   But they ain't none of mine.
   Hot tamales and they red hot.
   Yes, she got 'em for sale.
   I mean, yes she got 'em for sale, yes, yeah.

3. Hot tamales and they're red hot.
   Yes, she got 'em for sale.
   Hot tamales and they're red hot.
   Yes, she got 'em for sale.
   I got a letter from a girl in the room,
   Now she got somethin' good
   She got to bring home soon, now.
   It's hot tamales and they're red hot.
   Yes, she got 'em for sale.
   I mean, yes, she got 'em for sale, yeah.

4. Hot tamales and they're red hot.
   Yes, she got 'em for sale.
   Hot tamales and they're red hot.
   Yes, she got 'em for sale.
   They're too hot, boy!
   The billy goat back in a bumble bee nest.
   Ever since that, he can't take his rest, yeah.
   Hot tamales and they're red hot.
   Yeah, you got 'em for sale.
   I mean, yes, she got 'em for sale, yeah.

5. Hot tamales and they're red hot.
   Yes, she got 'em for sale.
   Man, don't mess around 'em hot tamales, now,
   'Cause they too black bad.
   If you mess around 'em hot tamales
   I'm 'onna upset your backbone,
   Put your kidneys to sleep.
   I'll due to break 'way your liver
   And dare your heart to beat 'bout my
   Hot tamales 'cause they're red hot.
   Yes, she got 'em for sale.
   I mean, yes, she got 'em for sale, yeah.

6. Hot tamales and they're red hot.
   Yes, she got 'em for sale.
   Hot tamales and they're red hot.
   Yes, she got 'em for sale.
   You know grandma laughs, and now grandpa, too.
   Well, I wonder what in the world
   We chillun gon' do, now.
   Hot tamales and they're red hot.
   Yes, she got 'em for sale.
   I mean, yes, she got 'em for sale, yeah.

7. Hot tamales and they're red hot.
   Yes, she got 'em for sale.
   Hot tamales and they're red hot.
   Yes, she got 'em for sale.
   Me and my babe bought a V-8 Ford.
   Well, we wind that thing
   All on the runnin' board, yes.
   Hot tamales and they're red hot.
   Yes, she got 'em for sale.
   I mean, yes, she got 'em for sale, yeah.

8. Hot tamales and they're red hot.
   Yes, she got 'em for sale. *They're too hot, boy!*
   Hot tamales and they're red hot.
   Yes, now, she got 'em for sale.
   You know the monkey, now the baboon playin' in the grass.
   Well, the monkey stuck his finger
   In that old "Good Gulf Gas," now.
   Hot tamales and they're red hot.
   Yes, she got 'em for sale.
   I mean, yes, she got 'em for sale, yeah.

9. Hot tamales and they're red hot.
   Yes, she got 'em for sale.
   Hot tamales and they're red hot.
   Yes, she got 'em for sale.
   I got a girl, sat she long and tall.
   Now, she sleeps in the kitchen
   With her feets in the hall, yes.
   Hot tamales and they're red hot.
   Yes, now, she got 'em for sale.
   I mean, yes, she got 'em for sale, yeah.

32-20 Blues

Words and Music by Robert Johnson

Key of A

G tuning, capo II:
(5th-1st) G-D-G-B-D

Intro

Moderately fast ♩ = 162

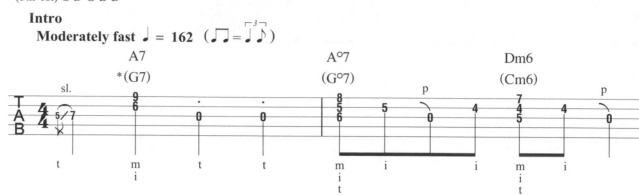

*Symbols in parentheses represent chord names respective to capoed banjo.
Symbols above reflect actual sounding chords. Capoed fret is "0" in tab.

1. 'F I send

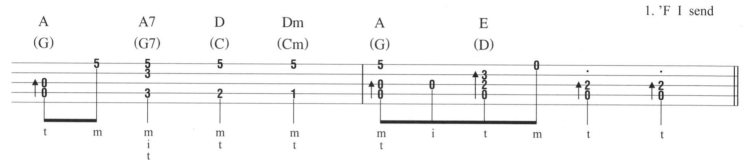

𝄋 Verse

for my baby,   and   she   don't   come,

3., 5. *See additional lyrics*

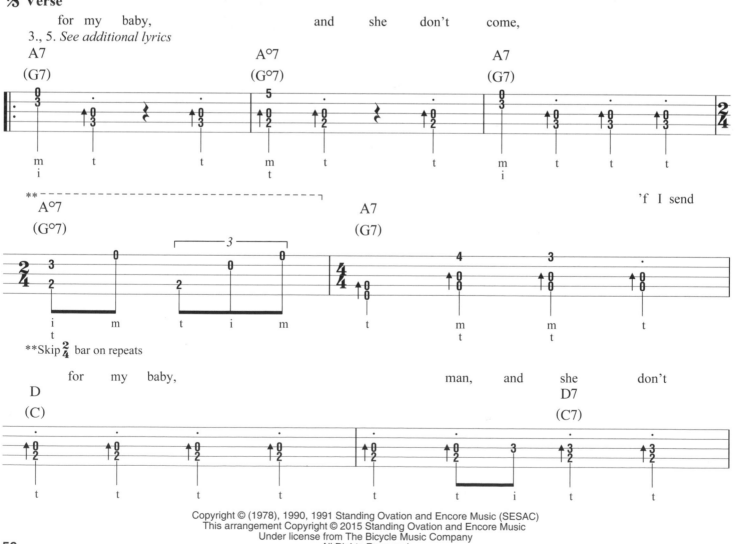

** Dashed line / 'f I send

**Skip 2/4 bar on repeats

for my baby,   man,   and   she   don't

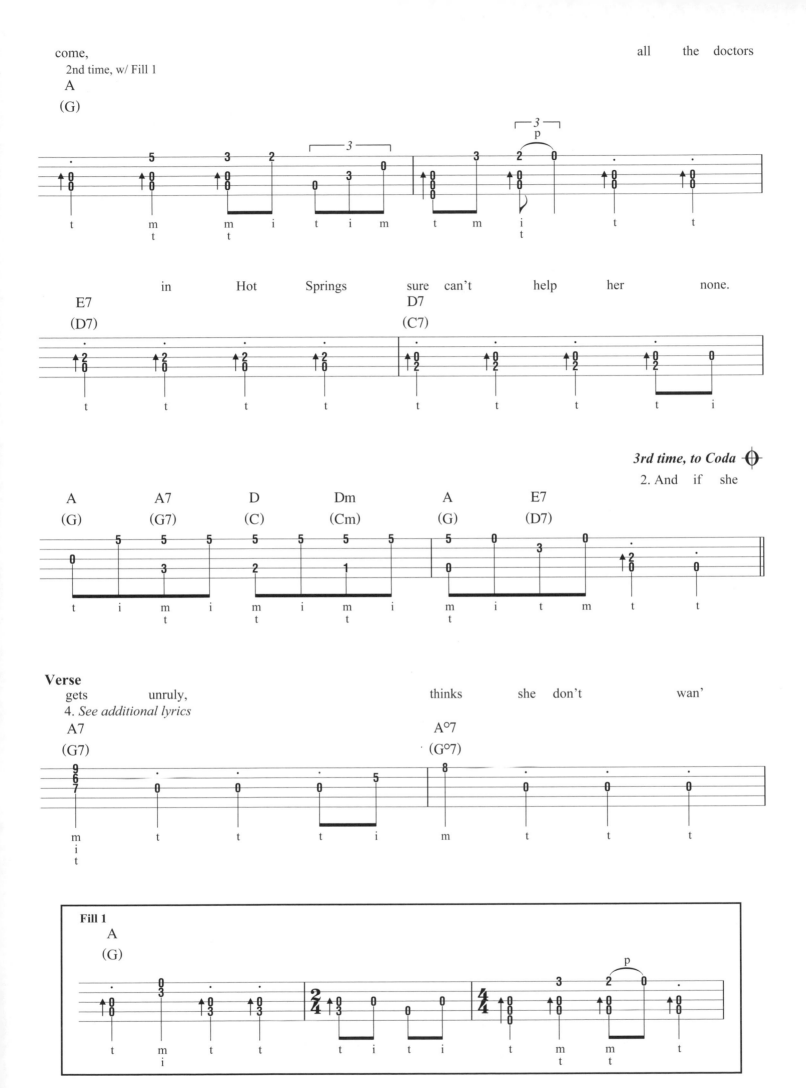

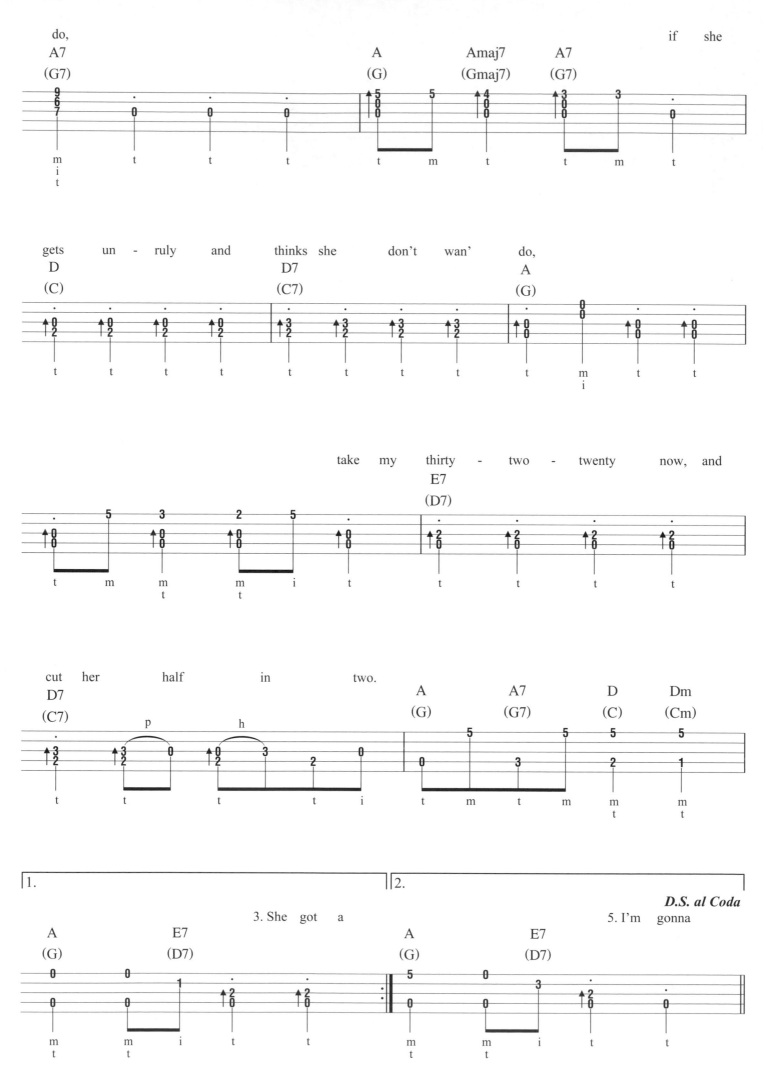

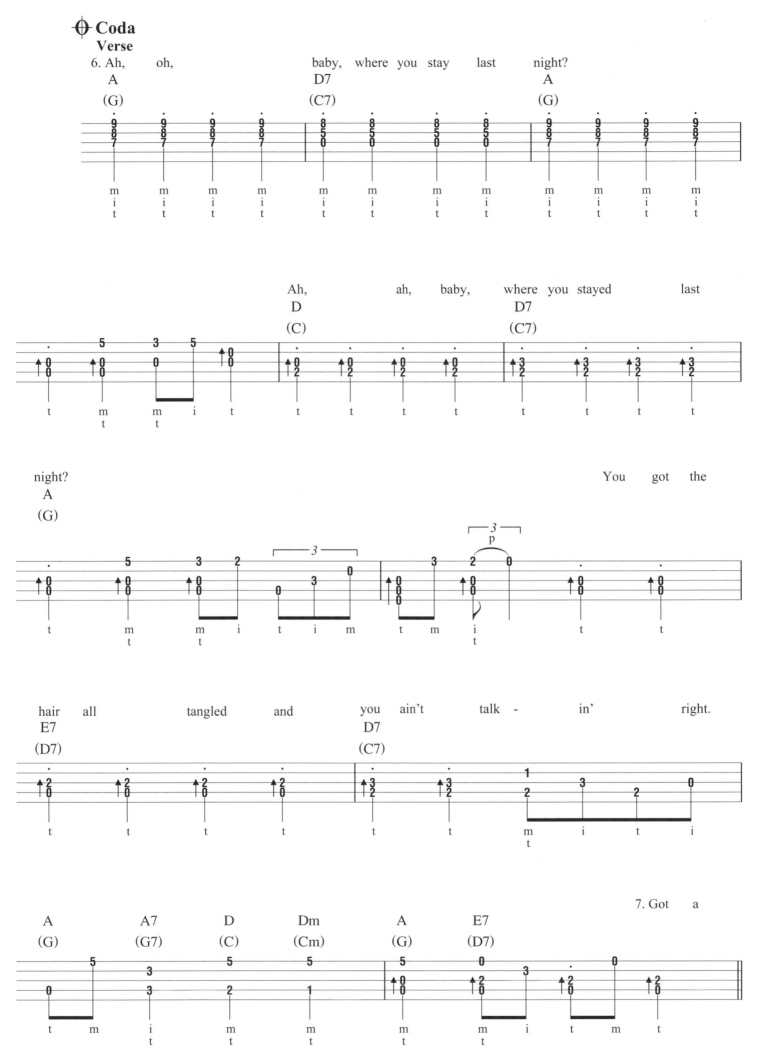

Verse

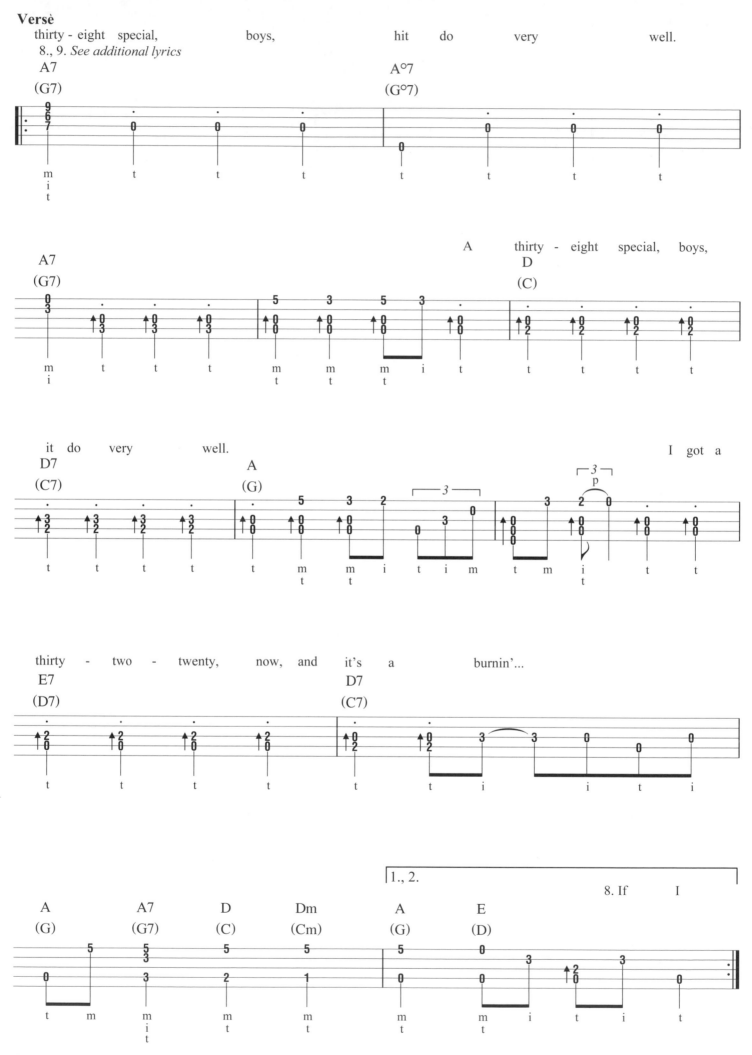

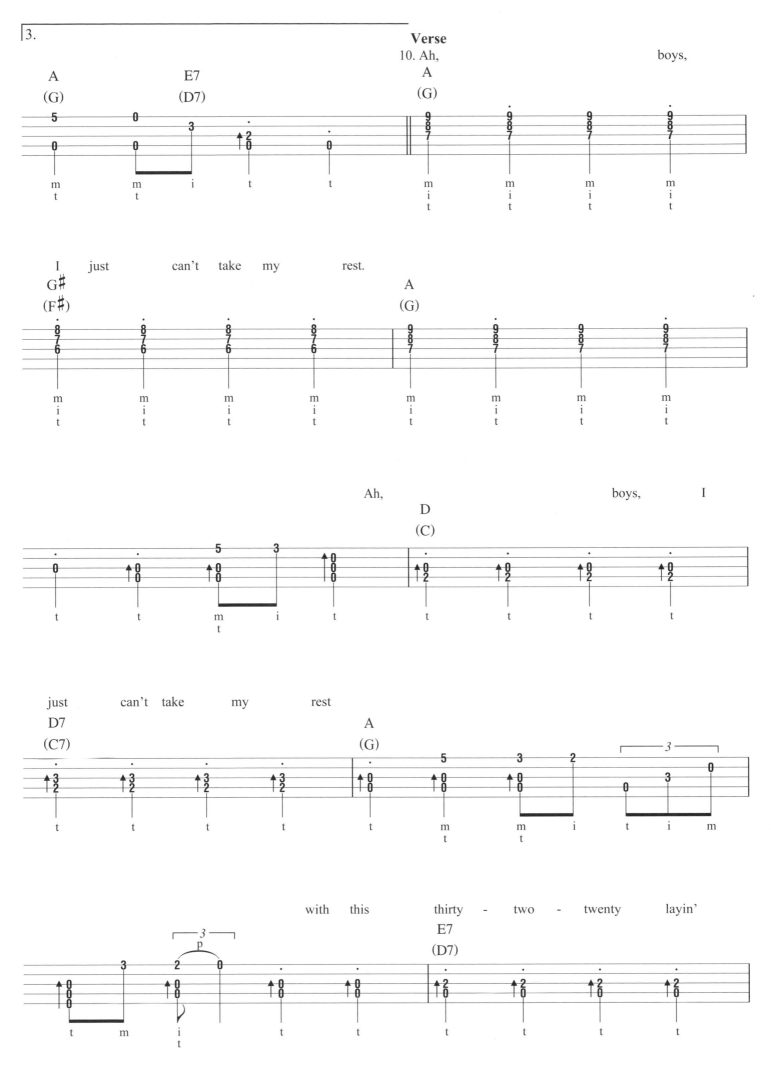

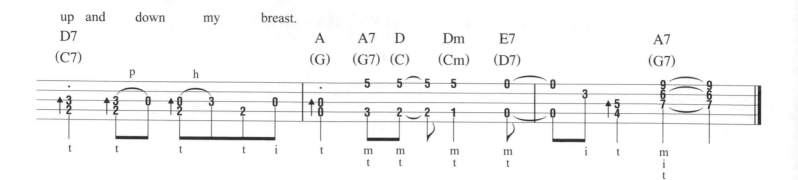

up and   down   my   breast.

Additional Lyrics

3. She got a thirty-eight special
   But I b'lieve it's most too light.
   She got a thirty-eight special
   But I b'lieve it's most too light.
   I got a thirty-two twenty,
   Got to make the camps alright.

4. If I send for my baby,
   Man, and she don't come,
   If I send for my baby,
   Man, and she don't come,
   All the doctors in Hot Springs
   Sure can't help her none.

5. I'm gonna shoot my pistol,
   Gonna shoot my Gatling gun.
   I'm 'onna shoot my pistol,
   Gotta shoot my Gatling gun.
   You made me love you,
   Now your man have come.

8. If I send for my baby,
   Man, and she don't come,
   If I send for my baby,
   Man, and she don't come,
   All the doctors in Wisconsin
   Sure can't help her none.

9. Hey, hey,
   Baby, where you stay last night?
   Hey, hey,
   Babe, where you stayed last night?
   You didn't come home
   Until the sun was shinin' bright.

Ramblin' on My Mind

(take 1)

Words and Music by Robert Johnson

Key of F#

G6 tuning, down 1/2 step:
(5th-1st) F#-C#-F#-A#-D#

Intro

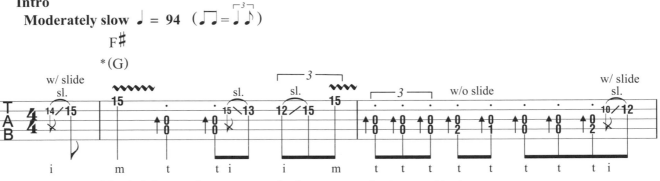

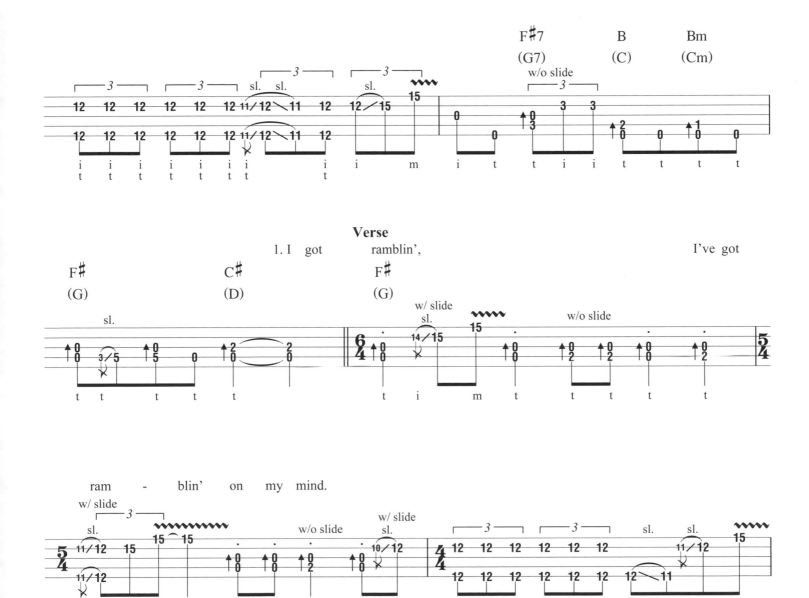

*Symbols in parentheses represent chord names respective to capoed banjo.
Symbols above reflect actual sounding chords. Capoed fret is "0" in tab.

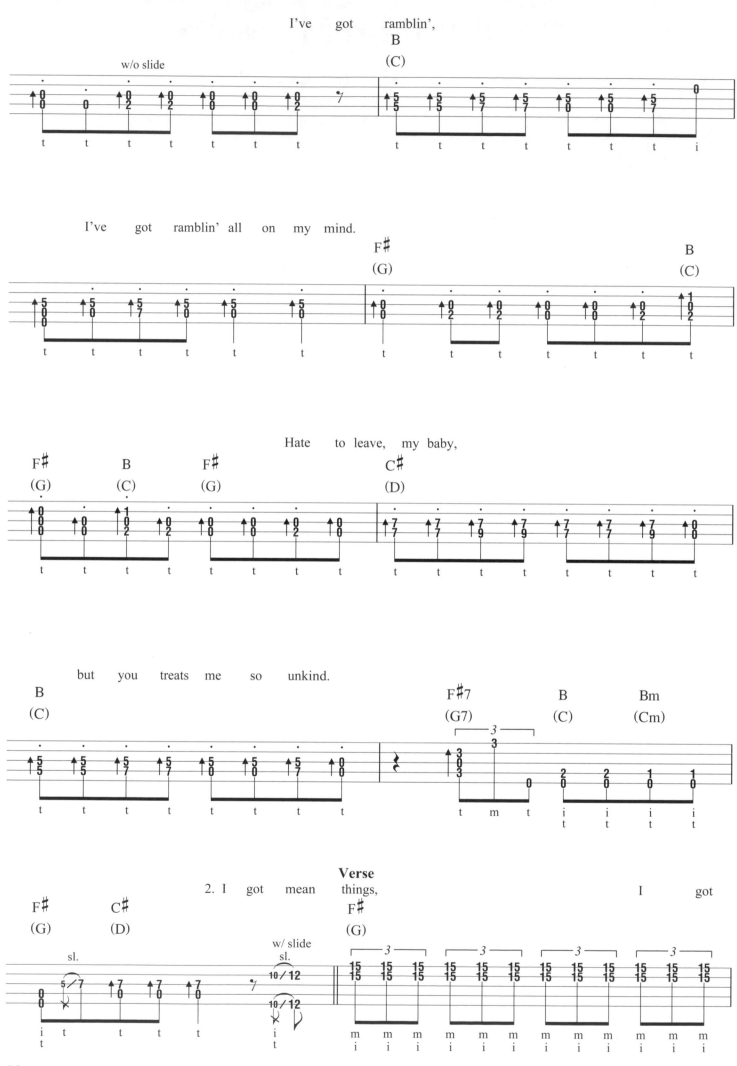

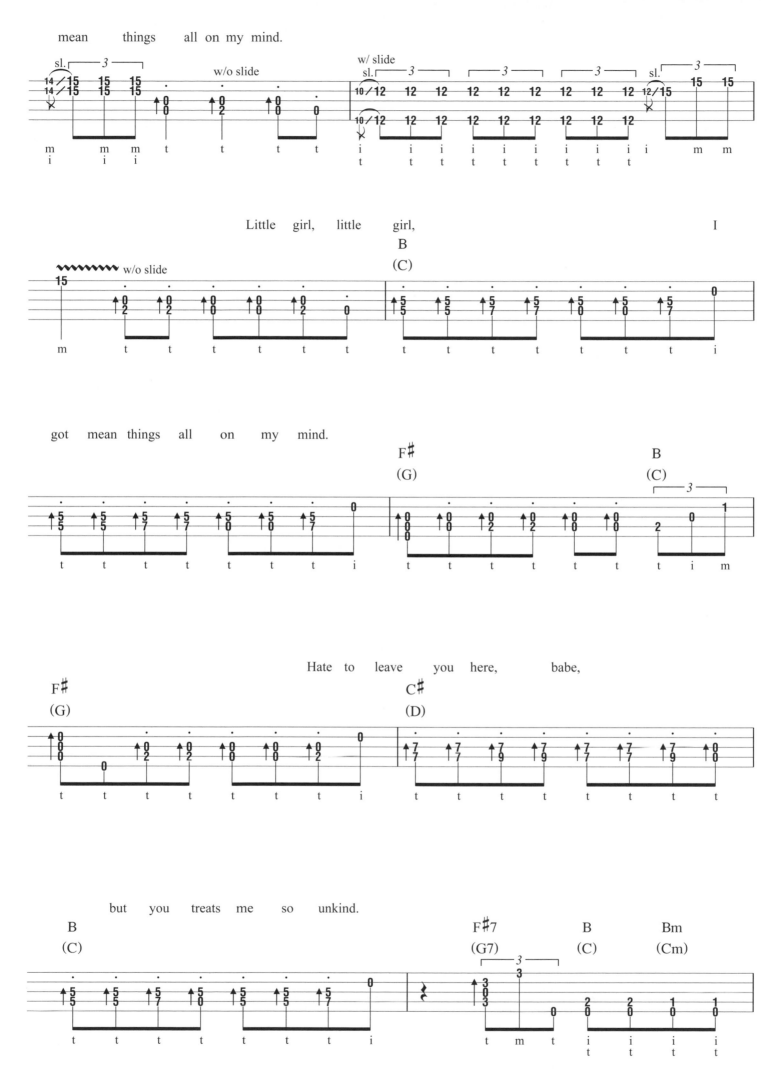

Verse

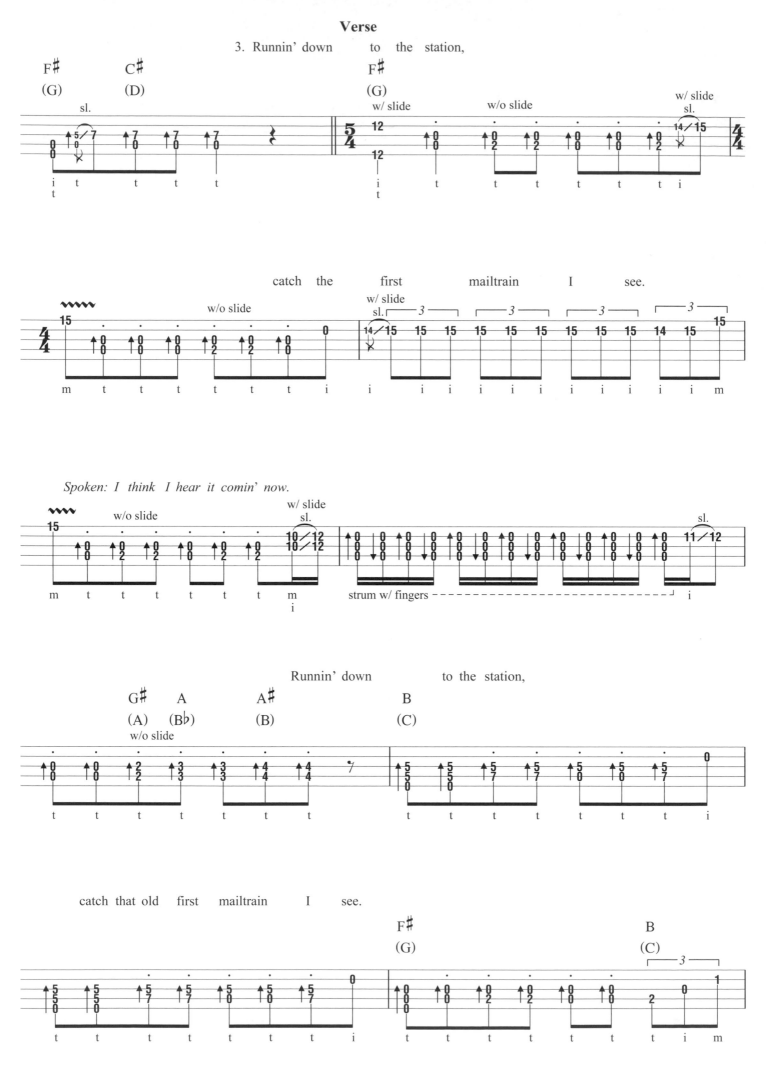

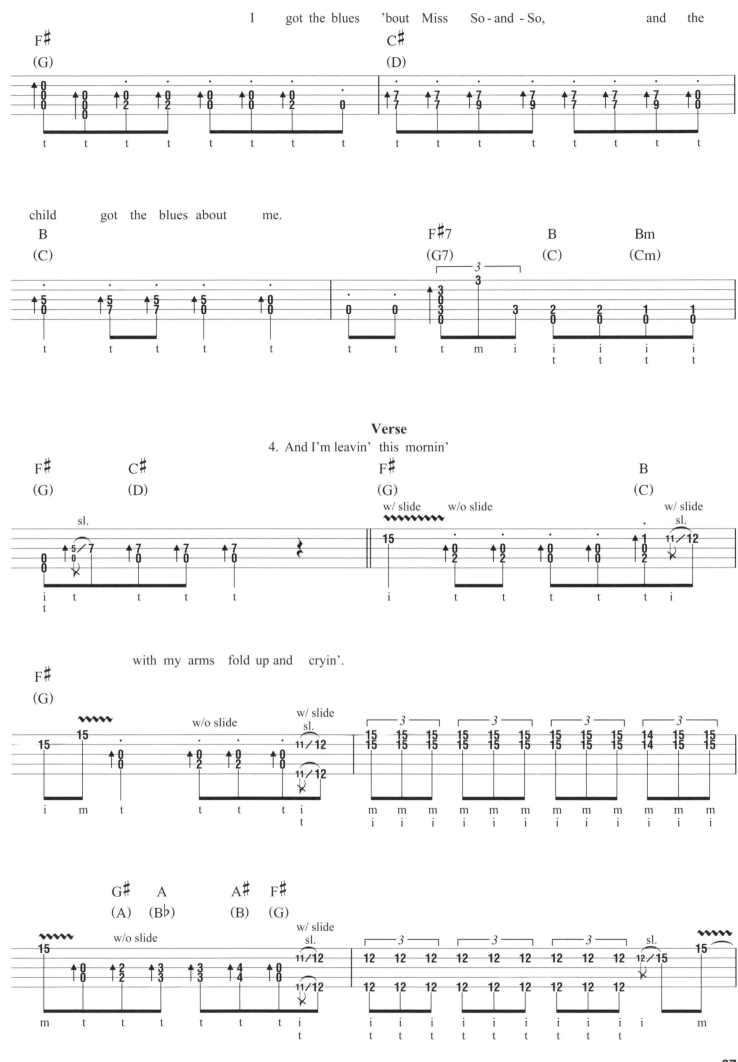

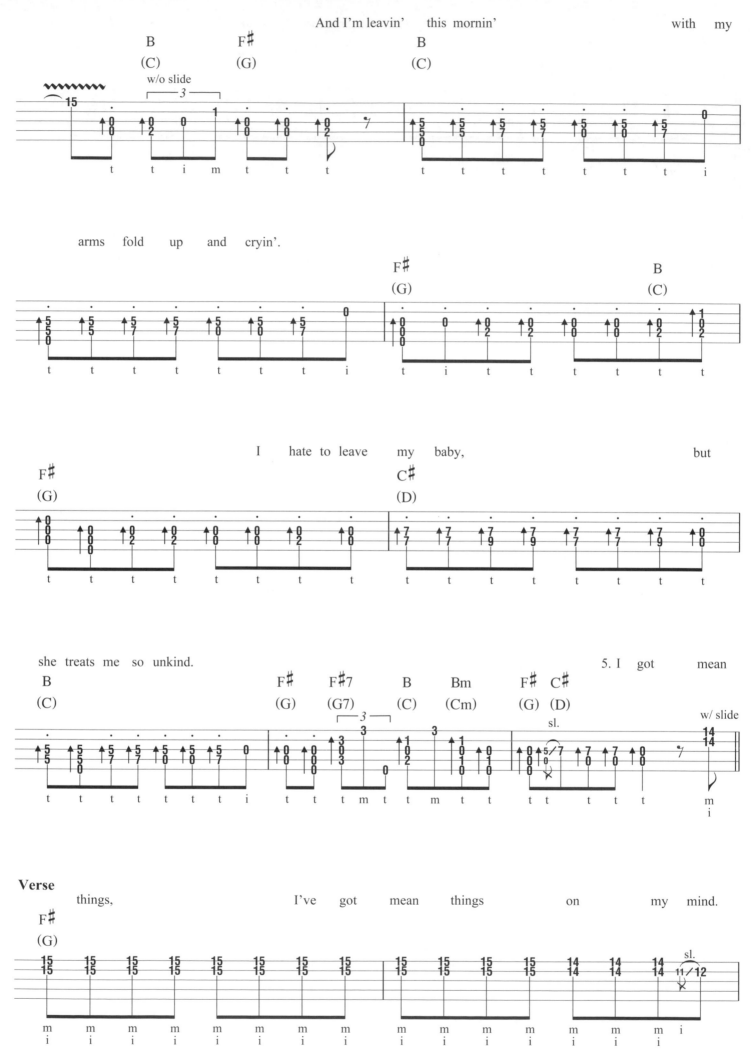

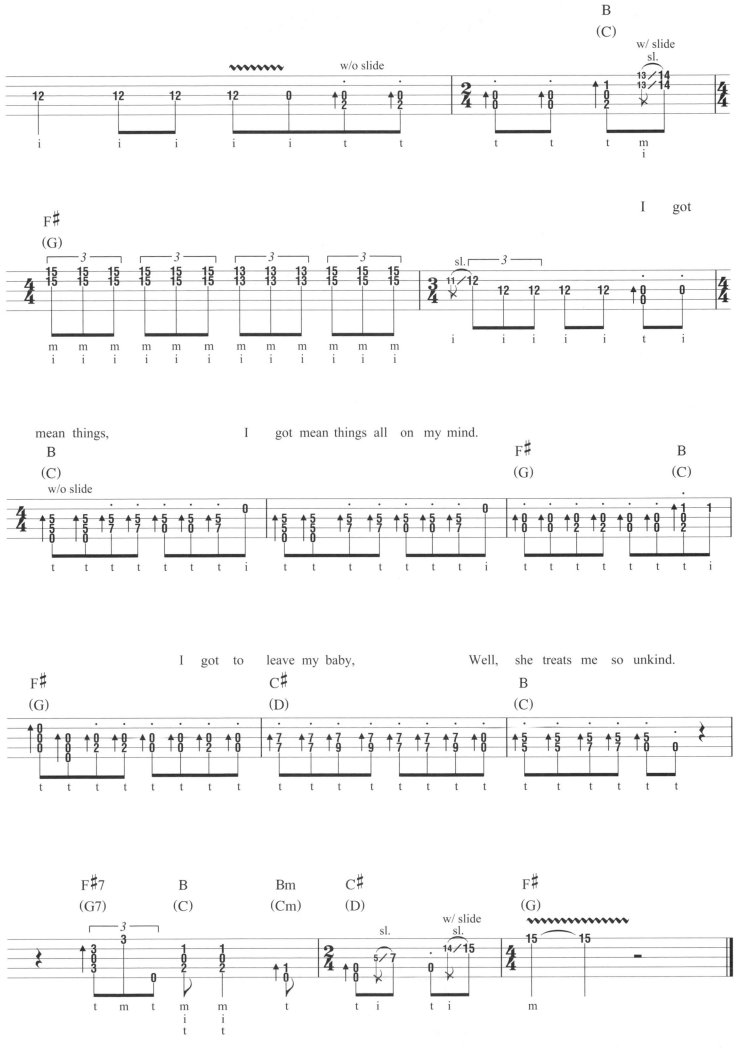

Walkin' Blues

Words and Music by Robert Johnson

Key of B

G tuning, capo IV:
(5th-1st) G-D-G-B-D

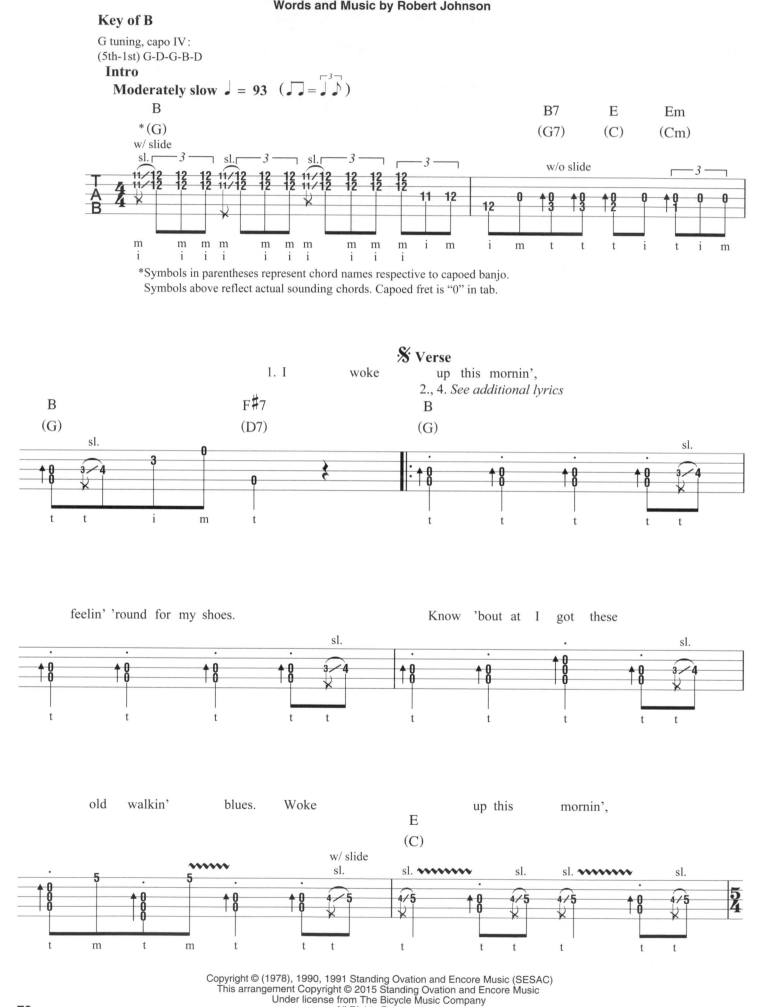

*Symbols in parentheses represent chord names respective to capoed banjo.
Symbols above reflect actual sounding chords. Capoed fret is "0" in tab.

This arrangement Copyright © 2015 Standing Ovation and Encore Music
Under license from The Bicycle Music Company
All Rights Reserved

feelin' 'round,   oh, for my shoes.

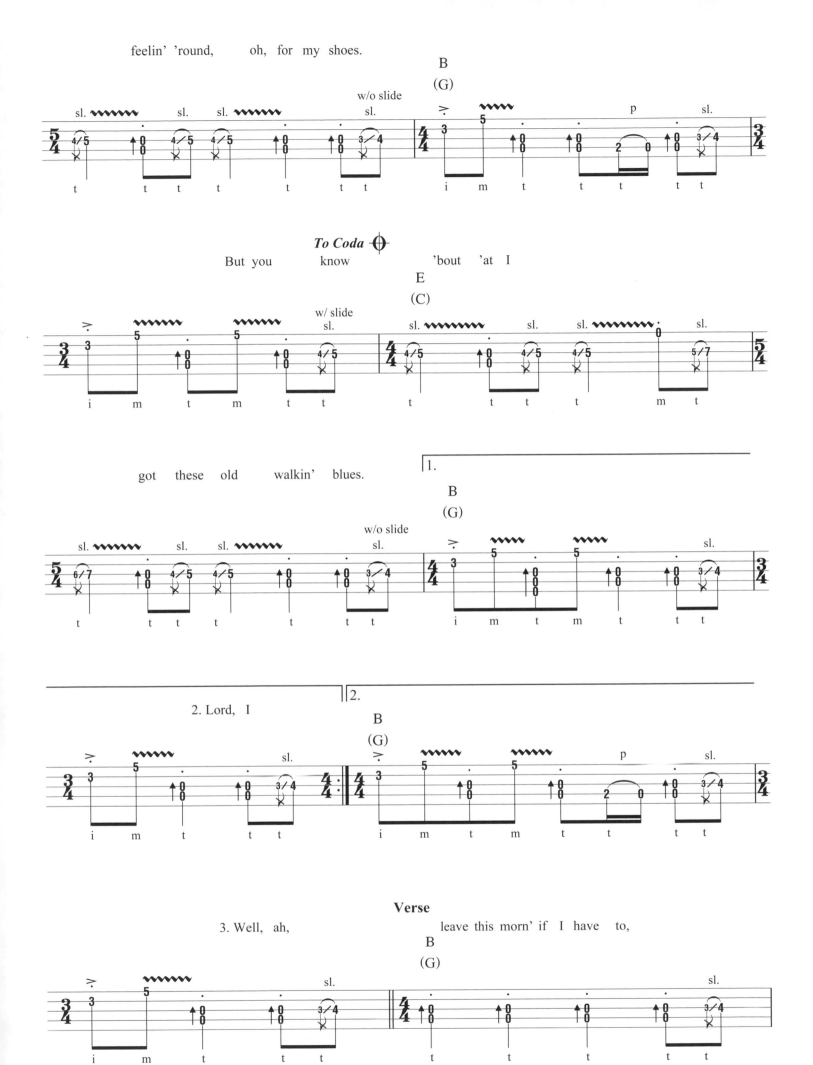

To Coda ⊕

But you   know   'bout 'at I

got these old   walkin' blues.

1.

2. Lord, I

Verse

3. Well, ah,   leave this morn' if I have   to,

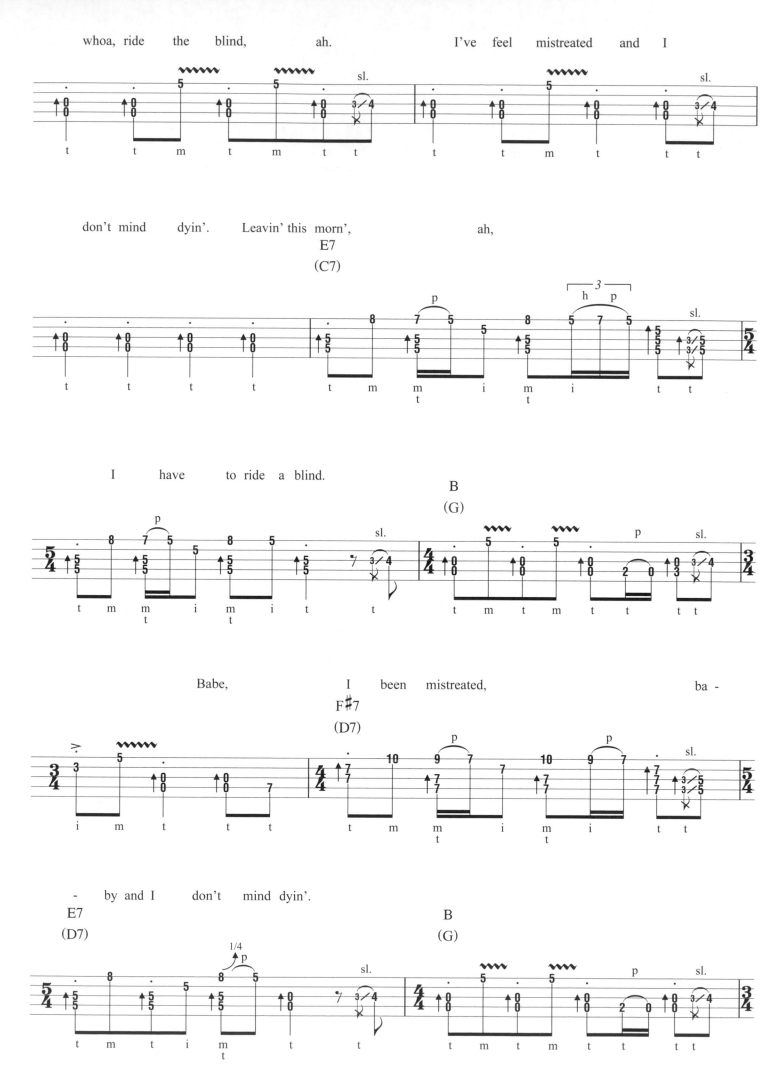

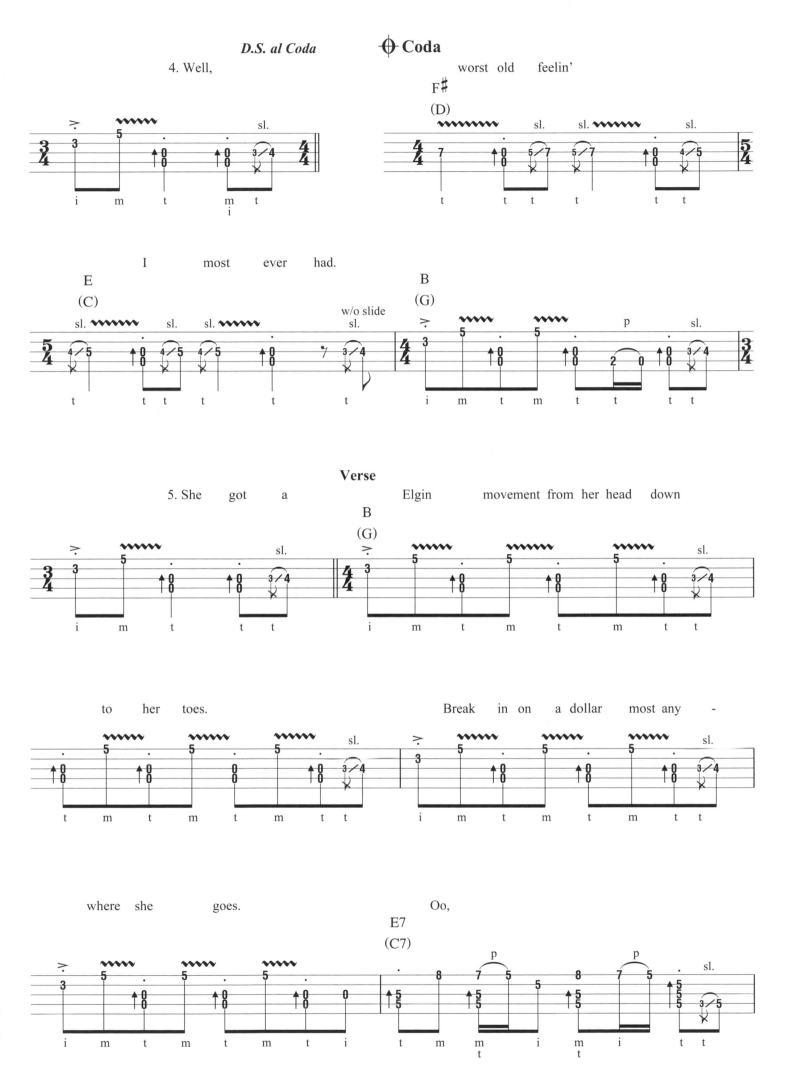

to her head   down   to her toes.   *Spoken: Oh, honey.*

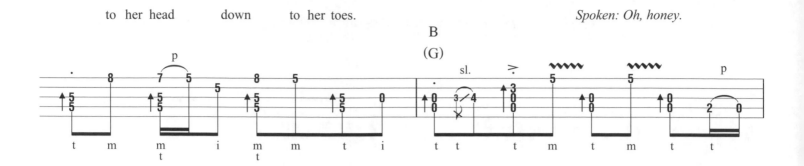

Lord,   she   break in on a dollar   most

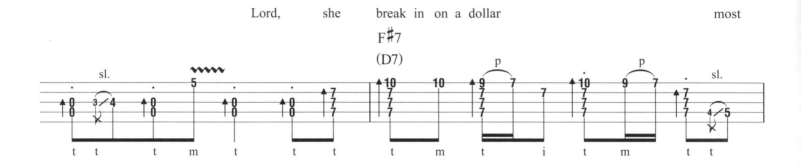

anywhere   she goes.

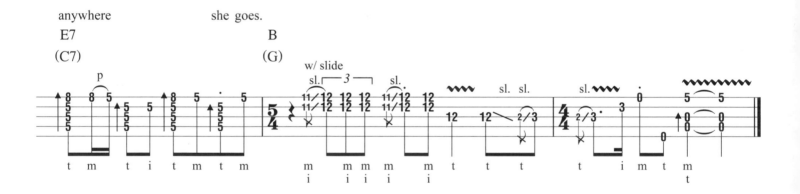

Additional Lyrics

2. Lord, I feel like blowin'
  My, whoa, old lonesome ho'n.
  Got up this mornin',
  My little Bernice was gone.
  Lord, I feel like blowin'
  My lonesome ho'n.
  Well, I got up this mornin',
  Whoa, all I had was gone.

4. Well, some people tell me
  That the worried blues ain't bad.
  Worst old feelin'
  I most ever had.
  Some people tell me
  That these old worried blues ain't bad.
  It's the worst old feelin'
  I most ever had.

BANJO NOTATION LEGEND

TABLATURE graphically represents the banjo fingerboard. Each horizontal line represents a string, and each number represents a fret.

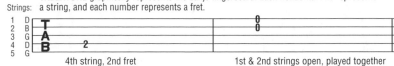

4th string, 2nd fret 1st & 2nd strings open, played together

TIME SIGNATURE:
The upper number indicates the number of beats per measure, the lower number indicates that a quarter note gets one beat.

CUT TIME:
Each note's time value should be cut in half. As a result, the music will be played twice as fast as it is written.

QUARTER NOTE:
time value = 1 beat

EIGHTH NOTES:
time value = 1/2 beat each
single   in series

SIXTEENTH NOTES:
time value = 1/4 beat each
single   in series

DOTTED QUARTER NOTE:
time value = 1 1/2 beat

TIE: Pick the 1st note only, then let it sustain for the combined time value.

TRIPLET: Three notes played in the same time normally occupied by two notes of the same time value.

GRACE NOTE: A quickly played note with no time value of its own. The grace note and the note following it only occupy the time value of the second note.

RITARD: A gradual slowing of the tempo or speed of the song.

QUARTER REST:
time value = 1 beat of silence

EIGHTH REST:
time value = 1/2 beat of silence

HALF REST:
time value = 2 beats of silence

WHOLE REST:
time value = 4 beats of silence

ENDINGS: When a repeated section has a first and second ending, play the first ending only the first time and play the second ending only the second time.

REPEAT SIGNS: Play the music between the repeat signs two times.

D.S. AL CODA:
Play through the music until you complete the measure labeled *"D.S. al Coda,"* then go back to the sign (𝄋). Then play until you complete the measure labeled *"To Coda ⊕ ,"* then skip to the section labeled *" ⊕ Coda."*

𝄋   *To Coda* ⊕   *D.S. al Coda*   ⊕ *Coda*

HAMMER-ON: Strike the first (lower) note with one finger, then sound the higher note (on the same string) with another finger by fretting it without picking.

PULL-OFF: Place both fingers on the notes to be sounded. Strike the first note and without picking, pull the finger off to sound the second (lower) note.

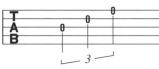

SLIDE UP: Strike the first note and then slide the same fret-hand finger up to the second note. The second note is not struck.

SLIDE DOWN: Strike the first note and then slide the same fret-hand finger down to the second note. The second note is not struck.

HALF-STEP CHOKE: Strike the note and bend the string up 1/2 step.

WHOLE-STEP CHOKE: Strike the note and bend the string up one step.

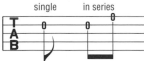

NATURAL HARMONIC: Strike the note while the fret-hand lightly touches the string directly over the fret indicated.

Harm.

BRUSH: Play the notes of the chord indicated by quickly rolling them from bottom to top.

Scruggs/Keith Tuners:

HALF-TWIST UP: Strike the note, twist tuner up 1/2 step, and continue playing.

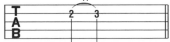

HALF-TWIST DOWN: Strike the note, twist tuner down 1/2 step, and continue playing.

WHOLE-TWIST UP: Strike the note, twist tuner up one step, and continue playing.

WHOLE-TWIST DOWN: Strike the note, twist tuner down one step, and continue playing.

Right Hand Fingerings

t = thumb   i = index finger   m = middle finger

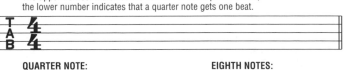

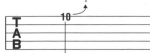

GREAT BANJO PUBLICATIONS
FROM HAL LEONARD CORPORATION

Hal Leonard Banjo Play-Along Series

1. BLUEGRASS

Ashland Breakdown • Deputy Dalton • Dixie Breakdown • Hickory Hollow • I Wish You Knew • I Wonder Where You Are Tonight • Love and Wealth • Salt Creek.
00102585 Book/CD Pack.....................$14.99

2. COUNTRY

East Bound and Down • Flowers on the Wall • Gentle on My Mind • Highway 40 Blues • If You've Got the Money (I've Got the Time) • Just Because • Take It Easy • You Are My Sunshine.
00105278 Book/CD Pack.....................$14.99

3. FOLK/ROCK HITS

Ain't It Enough • The Cave • Forget the Flowers • Ho Hey • Little Lion Man • Live and Die • Switzerland • Wagon Wheel.
00119867 Book/CD Pack.....................$14.99

4. OLD-TIME CHRISTMAS

Away in a Manger • Hark! the Herald Angels Sing • Jingle Bells • Joy to the World • O Holy Night • O Little Town of Bethlehem • Silent Night • We Wish You a Merry Christmas.
00119889 Book/CD Pack.....................$14.99

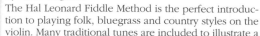